Meditating with Scripture

JOHN'S GOSPEL

Text copyright © Elena Bosetti 2010
The author asserts the moral right
to be identified as the author of this work

Published by
The Bible Reading Fellowship
15 The Chambers, Vineyard
Abingdon OX14 3FE
United Kingdom
Tel: +44 (0)1865 319700
Email: enquiries@brf.org.uk
Website: www.brf.org.uk
BRF is a Registered Charity

ISBN 978 1 84101 823 2

First published in the USA under the title *A Contemplative Reading of the Gospel: John* by Pauline
Books & Media, 50 Saint Paul's Avenue, Boston, MA 02130-3491
Website: www.pauline.org
Pauline Books & Media is the publishing house of the Daughters of St Paul, an international
congregation of women religious serving the Church with the communications media.
'P' and PAULINE are registered trademarks of the Daughters of St Paul.

This edition published 2010
10 9 8 7 6 5 4 3 2 1 0
All rights reserved

Acknowledgments
Unless otherwise stated, scripture quotations are taken from the New Revised Standard
Version Bible: Catholic Edition, copyright © 1989, 1993, Division of Christian Education
of the National Council of the Churches of Christ in the United States of America. Used by
permission. All rights reserved.

Texts of the New Testament used in this work are taken from The New Testament: St Paul
Catholic Edition, translated by Mark A. Wauck, copyright © 2000 by the Society of St Paul,
Staten Island, New York, and are used by permission. All rights reserved.

A catalogue record for this book is available from the British Library
Printed in Singapore by Craft Print International Ltd

Meditating with Scripture

JOHN'S GOSPEL

Elena Bosetti

To my dearest Agnese

※

CONTENTS

✳

INTRODUCTION

How should we read the Gospel of John? There are so many ways. The one presented here is rooted in an experience that does not separate reason from faith or the intellect from the heart. It follows the method of *lectio divina*, proposes a prayerful listening to the word, and is moved by the invocation of the Spirit. We cannot fly on eagle's wings unless the Spirit lifts us.

It is no accident that Christian tradition symbolises the fourth evangelist with an eagle. John is someone who flies high. Like the eagle, he soars into the highest heavens and gazes upon the sun. In the immensity of silence, he hears the unutterable Word, the dazzling source of life, which illuminates every living being. This light is dramatically opposed but never overcome, as the present tense of the verb emphasises: the light continues to shine in the darkness (John 1:5). And so it does today, for every one of us.

The Word that John goes on to exalt at length is entirely oriented toward the One who pronounces it: it is the Word of life that continually expresses eternal love. 'There is one God, who manifested himself through Jesus Christ his son, who is *his Word proceeding from silence*, who in all respects was well-pleasing to him that sent him.'[1]

So let us invoke the Holy Spirit so that we may enter into the dynamics of this Gospel written with a precise intention: '. . . so you may believe that Jesus is the Messiah, the Son of God, and that by believing you may have life in his name' (John 20:31).

The Gospels are not neutral works. They were born from faith and are intended to lead their hearers to faith. They were written from a unique perspective, in the light of the crucified and risen Lord. This light illuminates the Gospels from start to finish. John makes this outlook his theme, the interpretive key of his entire work.[2] He witnesses to the astonishment and the immense joy of those who have seen, heard, and touched 'what was from the beginning... the word of life' (1 John 1:1). He is the witness who recounts the indescribable experience opened to the believer's gaze in the tremendous scene of Golgotha, an experience transfigured in the light of the risen Jesus, who at the high point of the Gospel story induces the doubting disciple to exclaim, 'My Lord and my God!' (John 20:28).

We are invited to enter into this story and to search actively for the One who reveals himself. Many titles describe him: he is the *Logos*/Word, the Only Begotten, the Son of God, the Lamb of God, the Son of Man, the Messiah, the Good Shepherd, the King of Israel. He is the Light, the Living Water, the Bread come down from heaven, the Sheep Gate. He is the Way, the Truth, the Life, the Resurrection. It is impossible to remain indifferent to him. Readers can see themselves in the various personalities who appear in the story and interact with Jesus: 'representative individuals like Nicodemus, surprising individuals like the Samaritan woman and the adulterous woman, courageous witnesses like the man born blind. Then there are others who were closer to Jesus, like his mother, Mary Magdalene, Mary of Bethany, and Martha. Finally, there are his everyday companions, like Simon Peter, Thomas, Nathanael, the disciple whom Jesus loved, and even Judas, who was to betray him. Jesus' encounters with these figures transmit a multi-faceted Christology narrative.'[3]

Tradition identifies John as the disciple who rested his head on Jesus' chest at the Last Supper. He enjoyed a singular intimacy with the Master, but he does not covet his privileges. He desires, instead, to include us: '[W]hat we have seen and heard we also proclaim to you so you too may be in fellowship with us. Our fellowship is with the Father and with His Son, Jesus Christ, and we are writing these things so that our joy may be complete' (1 John 1:3–4). This is the good news; this is the joy that overflows!

So now let us begin, with gratitude and joy, our journey through the Gospel of John. This book is not an exhaustive commentary. It limits itself to offering a few notes for *lectio divina*, appropriate for personal use or in Bible study groups. The aim of this book is to soar on eagle's wings towards the contemplation of the Word made flesh—but beginning with the flesh, meaning the concrete structure of the text. The spiritual is not above or outside, but within, in all the depth and breadth of the word.

Our approach to *lectio divina* is inspired by the *Way, Truth, and Life* methodology proposed by Father James Alberione, the founder of the Pauline Family, a worldwide Christian community with particular dedication to following the example of St Paul in spreading the gospel by all means possible. So every chapter will be divided into three parts:

- Listening to the Word (Truth)
- Dialoguing with the Word (Way)
- Pause to ponder (Life)

✳

Chapter 1

JOHN THE BAPTIST
AND THE LAMB OF GOD

John the Baptist is a figure of unique importance among the personalities of the fourth Gospel, not only because he is the first to enter the scene, but also because of the quality of his testimony. The evangelist is so keenly aware of this that he includes his witness in the prologue, the meditation on the *Logos*/Word. If the Word is the light, then John, like a mirror, simply reflects the light from him:

There was a man sent by God named John.
He came as a witness to bear witness concerning the light,
so that all might believe through him.
He was not the light, but came to bear witness concerning the light. (John 1:6–8)

John reflects the light, but he does not do this silently: he speaks. He is the 'voice' that cries out in the desert. The first testimony he gives is set in Bethany beyond the Jordan and takes place over the course of three days.

John does not say everything in one day because he respects the time needed for his hearers to assimilate and understand his message more deeply. But in the device of the 'three days', we can discover another aspect that transcends *krónos* (earthly time) and points instead to the biblical concept of *kairós*—the decisive moment, the eschatological time of salvation. In this sense, these first 'three days' foreshadow the culminating days of Christ's

Passover, when the testimony of the Baptist—'behold the Lamb of God'—finds its complete fulfilment.

IN BETHANY BEYOND THE JORDAN:
THE FIRST THREE DAYS

Read the text of John 1:19–39, observing John's testimony and the characters who appear during the three days covered by the account. The action all takes place in a single setting: Bethany beyond the Jordan. Day by day the light becomes increasingly clear.

(The first day)
And this was John's witness when the Jews of Jerusalem sent priests and Levites to ask him, 'Who are you?'

He stated plainly and did not deny it, and he stated plainly, 'I am not the Messiah.'

'Then what are you?' they asked him. 'Are you Elijah?' 'I am not,' he said. 'Are you the Prophet?' 'No,' he answered.

So they said to him, 'Who are you? Give us an answer for those who sent us! What do you say about yourself?'

He said, *'I am the voice of one crying out in the desert, "Make straight the way of the Lord,"* as Isaiah the prophet said.'

There were also some who had been sent from the Pharisees, and they asked him, 'Then why do you baptise if you are neither the Messiah nor Elijah nor the Prophet?'

John answered them by saying, 'I baptise with water; among you stands one you do not know, the one who comes after me, the strap of whose sandal I am not worthy to untie.'

These things took place at Bethany beyond the Jordan, where John was baptising.

The next day he saw Jesus coming toward him and said, 'Here is the Lamb of God who takes away the sin of the world!

'This is the one of whom I said, "After me comes a man who is above me, because he was before me."'

'I did not know him; instead, I came baptising with water for this reason—so he might be revealed to Israel.'

Then John bore witness and said, 'I saw the Spirit descending like a dove from Heaven, and it remained upon him.

'I did not know him, but He Who sent me to baptise with water, He said to me, "Whoever you see the Spirit descending upon and remaining upon, he is the one who baptises with the Holy Spirit."

'And I have seen and have borne witness that this is the Son of God.'

The next day John was again standing there, as well as two of his disciples, and, as Jesus walked by, John looked right at him and said, 'Here is the Lamb of God.'

His two disciples heard him speaking and they followed Jesus.

When Jesus turned and saw them following him he said to them, 'What are you looking for?' So they said to him, 'Rabbi'—which, translated, means 'Teacher'—'where are you staying?'

'Come and you will see,' he said to them. So they came and saw where he was staying, and they stayed with him that day; it was about four in the afternoon. (1:19–39)

The Baptist's testimony is divided over three days:

- On the first day, John meets the delegation of religious leaders sent from Jerusalem, and denies that he is the Messiah. He identifies himself as a 'voice' in the perspective of the second part of Isaiah (Isaiah 40:3). As such he announces the one who is to come and who in fact is 'among you' (John 1:26). The Messiah is already present—he is in their midst—much as the risen Jesus will be described in John 20:19–22 and as the Lamb is presented in Revelation 5:6. The Messiah is present, but not recognised; he is present, but hidden.

- On the second day, the light grows more clear. The Baptist is the first to recognise the hidden Christ, and he points him out in symbolic, mysterious language: 'Here is the Lamb of God who takes away the sin of the world!' John, the 'voice', expresses himself at length during this second day. He says that Jesus 'was before me', that he 'baptises with the Holy Spirit'; he calls him 'the Son of God' (1:30, 33–34). And the reaction to this rich testimony is silence. No one speaks, no one objects. Silence falls upon the Hidden Christ revealed by John.
- On the third day, something new happens. John now sees Jesus passing by, but John seems to stop him with a look and a gesture, even before he says, 'Here is the Lamb of God' (1:36). What does this mean? John does not explain. But at least two of his disciples (Andrew and another whose name is not mentioned) must have intuited the meaning of this term because they immediately leave the Baptist to follow the Lamb—a new development on this third day. John's testimony, now condensed into a single striking phrase, sets in motion a new journey in the footsteps of Jesus.

The third day, therefore, marks a transition from the Baptist to the Lamb. The day continues with the disciples following Jesus, and it culminates in their staying and living together with him.

It is an unforgettable day, the memory of which remains vivid years later. It begins a transforming experience, which cannot be guarded jealously but must be shared. As Mary Magdalene will later run to the apostles, Andrew runs to find his brother Simon and proclaims to him enthusiastically, 'We have found the Messiah!' (1:41). The wait has ended; he who was to come has now arrived.[1]

WHAT KIND OF MESSIAH IS HE?

We should note that Andrew does not repeat the Baptist's exact words: he does not say to his brother, 'We have found the Lamb of God!' Only the Baptist uses this title. It is not found anywhere else in the Gospel except in an allusive way in the great scene of Golgotha, at the death of Jesus (see John 19:36).

Although Jesus loved to speak with images and presents himself as the Sheep Gate and as the Good Shepherd, he never says of himself, 'I am the Lamb of God.' Why not? Did he perhaps want to distance himself from the meaning the Baptist gave to this expression? This intriguing question deserves further study, but one thing seems clear: apart from the meaning that it might have had in the Baptist's mind, for the evangelist John the title 'Lamb of God' is a decisive hermeneutical key. He uses it for interpreting Christ's identity and mission, which is fully revealed at the very end, when he is lifted up on the cross and pierced through.

THE BIBLICAL BACKGROUND

Against the backdrop of the Jewish biblical tradition, the designation 'Lamb of God' may have held a variety of associations and connections for John the Baptist's audience. Here are five of them:

1. **The lamb of the burnt offering.** The expression 'Lamb of God' can be understood as the lamb that God himself provides, that belongs to him and is given by him. In the account of Genesis, Isaac asks, 'The fire and the wood are here, but where is the lamb for a burnt offering?' (22:7). Abraham does not have the heart to reveal to his son what is in store for him, and so he replies inconclusively, 'God himself will provide the lamb for a burnt offering, my son' (v. 8). What follows shows that God truly does provide: 'And Abraham looked up and saw a ram, caught in a

thicket by its horns. Abraham went and took the ram and offered it up as a burnt offering instead of his son' (v. 13). According to the tradition of the Jewish *targumim*, or commentary on the Hebrew texts, the lamb/ram that is substituted for Isaac is a prefiguring of both the Passover lamb and the lamb of the *Tamid* (see point 3 below).

2. **The Passover lamb.** This lamb had to be not only without blemish, just like everything else that is offered to God, but also young, 'a year-old' (Exodus 12:5). The Passover lamb represents life in all its freshness and innocence and is associated with the great liberation, the Passover of the Lord, the exodus from Egypt (see Exodus 12:11).

3. **The lamb of the *Tamid*.** The lamb of the daily (*Tamid*) sacrifice also had to be without blemish and was burnt in the temple to pay for personal and communal sins. And the Baptist, identifying Jesus as the 'Lamb of God', makes explicit reference to sin: he is 'the Lamb of God who takes away the sin of the world!' (John 1:29). The first letter of John also develops along the same perspective: Jesus 'appeared to take away sins' (3:5).

4. **The lamb as a symbol for the prophet/suffering servant.** In Jeremiah 11:19, the lamb is a metaphor for the prophet's conduct, utterly without guile or malice, in clear contrast with the treachery of his opponents: 'But I was like a gentle lamb led to the slaughter. And I did not know it was against me that they devised schemes...' This image is taken up again in the poem of the suffering servant: 'He was oppressed, and he was afflicted, yet he did not open his mouth; like a lamb that is led to the slaughter, and like a sheep that before its shearers is silent, so he did not open his mouth' (Isaiah 53:7). According to the Lord's mysterious plan, the innocent servant-lamb bears upon himself the iniquities of others, and without rebelling he suffers their consequences. In this perspective, the lamb becomes a symbol of the meek and innocent Messiah who suffers violence and death. Is this how the Baptist thought about the reference?

The evangelist certainly held this perspective, together with that of the Passover lamb, but it may be too much to attribute it to the Baptist.

5. **The apocalyptic lamb.** The Baptist's preaching seems to correspond more closely to the figure of the lamb as seen in some apocalyptic texts, particularly in the Ethiopian Book of Enoch (a book accepted as part of scripture by the Ethiopian Orthodox Church) and in John's Revelation. There, the victorious lamb has 'seven horns', which expresses the fullness of divine power (Revelation 5:6). In this context the lamb is not simply meek. Instead, Revelation speaks paradoxically of 'the wrath of the Lamb' (6:16). This aspect may clarify the scene of the purification of the temple, where Jesus gives full expression to his disgust: '... making a whip out of rope, he drove them all out of the Temple, along with the sheep and the oxen. He poured out the moneychangers' coins and overturned their tables' (John 2:15).

When the Baptist sees this young man of about 30 walk by, a thrill of excitement runs through him: 'Here is the Lamb of God!' He is the man who was awaited, who was sought. 'This is the one of whom I spoke,' the Lord says to the prophet Samuel at Saul's arrival (1 Samuel 9:17). Similarly, when he sees Jesus, John cries out: 'Here is the Lamb of God!'

This 'here is' will return in the fourth Gospel at its most dramatic point. When Jesus comes before Pilate, scourged and crowned with thorns, Pilate will present him to the crowds with these words: 'Look at the man! ... Here is your king!' (John 19:5, 14). This man, mocked and humiliated for his messianic claims, appears as the silent Lamb of whom Isaiah speaks (53:7).

Later, in the great scene of Golgotha, the image of Christ as the Passover lamb emerges. Jesus is condemned to death while the lambs are being killed in the temple for the feast of Passover. In the evangelist's eyes, Jesus appears as the true Passover lamb, of which 'not a bone... shall be broken' (Exodus 12:46; John 19:36). In the end, what the Baptist was saying from the beginning becomes completely clear: 'Here is the Lamb of God who takes away the sin of the world!' (John 1:29).

The Gospel of John is therefore embraced by a twofold testimony: at the beginning, that of the Baptist; and at the end, that of the evangelist himself. He vouches personally for the authenticity of all the things he has recounted: 'And the one who saw it has borne witness and his witness is true, and he knows that he is speaking the truth so you, too, may believe' (John 19:35). Behold the Shepherd who lays down his life (see John 10:11), or rather, the Shepherd who becomes a Lamb! From his pierced heart issue blood and water—water that alludes to the Spirit, the source of life (see Zechariah 14:8; Ezekiel 47:1–12). All men and women of all time will look to him, irresistibly drawn by his love: 'And when I am lifted up from the earth I will draw all men to myself' (John 12:32).

DIALOGUING WITH THE WORD

Let us imagine ourselves in Bethany on the banks of the Jordan, among the people listening to the Baptist. He is 'the voice of one crying out in the desert', who invites his listeners to prepare the way of the Lord. What kind of room does his voice find within us, within the desert of our lives? Does it echo hollowly within us, or do we know how to listen to it?

John does not draw attention to himself. He is entirely focused upon the awaited Messiah, the Lamb. Later, when Jesus also begins baptising, prompting suspicion among the Baptist's disciples, he calms them:

'A man can receive nothing unless it's given to him from Heaven. You yourselves can bear witness to me that I said "I am not the Messiah," but instead said, "I am the one sent before him." The one who has the bride is the bridegroom. The friend of the bridegroom, who stands and listens to him, rejoices with joy at the bridegroom's voice. So in this my joy has been fulfilled. He must increase while I must decrease.' (John 3:27–30)

The great baptiser is not jealous; on the contrary, he is happy to have his disciples follow Jesus. In this sense, he is happy to 'decrease' so that Jesus may increase. The Bride, a symbol of the people of God, belongs to the Bridegroom, meaning Jesus. And John has no intention of violating that belonging. His joy, instead, lies in being the 'friend' of the Bridegroom, and of taking delight in his voice. Is our love for Jesus as free and as pure as this? How do we bear witness to him? Do we point him out so that others may follow him?

The two disciples accompanying the Baptist quickly welcome his testimony and immediately follow Jesus. They understand their teacher's instruction, and without hesitating they leave him to follow the Lamb of God. They want to stay with him, where he lives. And they are not disappointed. In fact, they will never forget that first meeting, and will even remember what time of day it was. Their readiness challenges the disciples of every generation, and challenges us, too, to take up the journey behind the Lamb of God, following in his footsteps.

How do we welcome the testimony of the Baptist? It resounds in every eucharistic celebration, appearing in the Gloria, the hymn of praise that precedes the proclamation of the word of God. In the Gloria, we say, 'Lamb of God, you take away the sin of the world, have mercy on us.' And before approaching the Eucharist, we invoke the Lamb of God again, as the one who takes away the sins of the world, our sins. What does it mean to follow Christ the Lamb in the context of a society that is often violent and oppressive?

✢

PAUSE TO PONDER

Let's allow ourselves to be drawn to the Lamb whom God especially loves and carries in his bosom (Isaiah 40:11; John 1:1–2). Let us thank him that he loved us to the point of shedding his blood and giving us the supreme gift of his life. Let us purify ourselves in his innocent blood. And let us sing to him, from the depths of our hearts, the hymn of praise from John's Revelation:

Worthy are you to take the scroll
and to open its seals,
because you were slain and by your blood
redeemed for God
a multitude from every tribe and tongue,
every people and nation.
You have made them a Kingdom, priests for our God,
and they shall rule over the earth...
Worthy is the Lamb who was slain to receive
power, wealth, wisdom, and might,
honour, glory, and blessing! (5:9–12)

✳

Chapter 2

JESUS AND THE FIRST DISCIPLES

The encounter with Jesus is contagious. The joy of having met
him cannot be kept secretly inside one's own heart—it must be
communicated and witnessed to. The third day thus illuminates the
days following it, giving rise to a surprising movement of followers
and disciples, as seen in John 1:40–51. We can divide this passage
into two parts, according to the indications of time provided by the
evangelist: the first part (vv. 40–42) takes place during the 'third
day', the day of the encounter between Jesus and John and his
disciples, culminating in Jesus' words to Peter; the second part
(vv. 43–51) takes place on 'the next day', and introduces a new
scenario determined by Jesus' decision to leave for Galilee.

(The day of the encounter)
Now Andrew, the brother of Simon Peter, was one of the two who
were listening to John and had followed him.

He first found his own brother, Simon, and said to him, 'We
have found the Messiah!'—which, translated, is 'Christ'.

He brought him to Jesus. Jesus gazed at him and said, 'You
are Simon son of John; you shall be called "Kephas"—which is
translated, 'Peter' (vv. 40–42).

The next day he decided to go to Galilee, and he found Philip. And
Jesus said to him, 'Follow me!'

Now Philip was from Bethsaida, from Andrew's and Peter's
city.

Philip found Nathanael and said to him, 'We have found the one Moses wrote about in the Torah, as well as the Prophets—Jesus son of Joseph from Nazareth!'

And Nathanael said to him, 'Can anything good come from Nazareth?' Philip said to him, 'Come and see!'

Jesus saw Nathanael coming toward him and said about him, 'Here is a true Israelite, in whom there is no guile!'

Nathanael said to him, 'Where do you know me from?' Jesus answered and said to him, 'Before Philip called you, while you were under the fig tree, I saw you.'

Nathanael answered him, 'Rabbi, you are the Son of God, you are the king of Israel!'

Jesus answered and said to him, 'Do you believe because I told you I saw you beneath the fig tree? You will see greater things than this!'

And he said to him, 'Amen, amen, I say to you, you will see *Heaven opened up and the angels of God ascending and descending upon the Son of Man!*' (vv. 43–51)

THE DAY OF THE ENCOUNTER
AND THE FOLLOWING DAY

See what happens when one encounters Jesus! Andrew could not keep to himself his joy at having met the awaited Messiah. He thus becomes, to use the symbolic language of Jesus, a 'fisher of men'. He doesn't have to go far. He goes fishing in the place closest to him, within his own family. He looks for his brother Simon, and tells him the incredible news, the astonishing discovery: 'We have found the Messiah!' And he immediately leads him to Jesus.

How does Simon react? He says nothing. Not a word comes from his mouth, neither in reply to Andrew nor to Jesus. The prince of the apostles, the one whom Jesus will call to 'feed his lambs' and 'tend his sheep' (see John 21:15–17), to guide his Church, makes a humble first appearance on the stage. He is willing to be guided and led to Jesus. The greatness of Simon Peter, as far as the Gospel writer is concerned, lies precisely in the way he trusts his brother.

Jesus does not waste time praising Andrew for his excellent powers of persuasion, but instead fixes his gaze on this new follower and gives him a new name. He will no longer be called Simon, but rather Cephas, or Peter, the rock. The construction of a house begins with its foundation on rock, and Jesus has found this rock in Simon Peter. Now they can get moving. A new day has begun.

While walking towards Galilee, Jesus meets Philip of Bethsaida (meaning 'house of fishing', a place where fish are found). This is obviously not a casual encounter, but one planned and sought by Jesus, who always takes the initiative. At the end, in the intimacy of the upper room, he will say to his disciples, 'You did not choose me; on the contrary, I chose you' (John 15:16). And Philip, in John's Gospel, is the first to whom Jesus directly addresses the invitation: 'Follow me!'

How does Philip react? He remains silent, like Peter. Not an objection, not a word. His prompt response is simply silence. Philip is almost mesmerised by Jesus and, drawn irresistibly, he follows him. But being silent does not mean that one cannot speak. Philip is silent with Jesus, but he does not hold back from talking about him, and he is no less persuasive than his friend Andrew. Just as Andrew leads his brother Simon to Jesus, so also Philip brings to him Nathanael, who certainly did not have a reputation for being gullible. Compared with Andrew's concise statement ('We have found the Messiah!'), Philip's is longer and more detailed: 'We have found the one Moses wrote about in the Torah, as well as the Prophets—Jesus son of Joseph from Nazareth!' As we will soon see, this message deserves to be explored in depth.

How does Nathanael react? At first, he responds in the negative. He is absolutely sceptical about the connection between the Messiah and the town of Nazareth. This assertion even seems to irritate him: 'Can anything good come from Nazareth?' Philip does not get caught in polemics, but responds to Nathanael's frankness in a rather pragmatic manner: 'Come and see.' Nathanael accepts this challenge. His openness and willingness to face the evidence are definite points in his favour.

Jesus welcomes Nathanael with a splendid compliment: 'Here's a true Israelite, in whom there is no guile!' The blunt, straightforward Nathanael responds: 'Where do you know me from?' Nathanael is not the type to be won over by compliments, and Jesus knows this. But the sign he mentions is so specific—'while you were under the fig tree, I saw you'—that Nathanael is stunned. He immediately proclaims that Jesus is the Messiah and the Son of God.

He was too quick in announcing this, the Master seems to say, adding, 'You will see greater things than this!' And he tells not only Nathanael, but also Philip and the other disciples of a marvellous sign that will manifest the glory of Jesus: 'Amen, amen, I say to you, you will see *Heaven opened up and the angels of God ascending and descending upon the Son of Man!*'

For people familiar with the scriptures, as Philip and Nathanael were, these words need no commentary. They allude to the dream of Jacob, when he spent the night in Bethel: 'And he dreamed that there was a ladder set up on the earth, the top of it reaching to heaven; and the angels of God were ascending and descending on it' (Genesis 28:12).

Just as Jacob/Israel did not know that God was in that place (Genesis 28:16), the disciples represented by Nathanael still do not realise that Jesus fulfils God's presence among men... He will not be king of Israel to exercise dominion like that of the kings of history, but for the greater fulfilment of man's nature, manifesting his love and glory with the gift of his own life. [1]

We should note how, in John's account, vocation is interwoven with mission. Called directly by Jesus, Philip leads Nathanael to him, as Andrew had led Simon. Three parts of this account strike me in a particular way: (1) the identification of Jesus, the Messiah, as the 'son of Joseph, from Nazareth'; (2) the invitation to 'Come and see'; and (3) the allusion to Jacob's ladder, which sounds like both a promise and a fulfilment.

SON OF JOSEPH FROM NAZARETH

Philip's presentation of Jesus astonishes Nathanael (and those whom he represents). This plain-spoken Israelite doesn't hesitate to display his difficulty in connecting the information offered by Philip: how is it possible that 'the one about whom Moses wrote, and the prophets'—the Messiah—could be the 'son of Joseph from Nazareth'? Nathanael expresses an opinion that was widespread among his countrymen: 'Can anything good come from Nazareth?' This remark certainly reflects some snobbery: the people of Cana, Nathanael's town, must have felt that they were far 'superior' to the people of Nazareth. But this is not simply a gibe—much more lies behind Nathanael's reaction. At issue is the scandal of the Messiah's humble origins.

The evangelist John does not gloss over this difficulty. After his marvellous hymn to the Word made flesh, the prologue, he now draws attention to a contrast: the Word of God is made flesh, and pitches his tent in an unknown, insignificant village like Nazareth. The Awaited One of Israel, the one of whom Moses and the prophets wrote, is the 'son of Joseph from Nazareth'. He is nobody special. He is a healthy, strong, sensitive and intelligent man, certainly, but not from high society, and not even from the Holy City. He receives neither preferential treatment nor honorary title, nor notoriety.

It is interesting to note that while the name of Jesus' mother never occurs in the fourth Gospel, the expression 'son of Joseph' appears twice (1:45, 6:42). The portion of the Gospel bracketed by these two occurrences could be titled: 'Who is Jesus, the son of Joseph?'[2]

As for the humble village of Nazareth, we now know more, thanks to archaeological excavations. It was undoubtedly a small village, but it was not as isolated as might be imagined. Nearby was the city of Sepphoris, which was strongly Hellenised. Excavations have revealed a fairly large Greek theatre that could seat more than 5000. This city must have provided a great deal of work for the craftsman or carpenter of Nazareth.[3] But we want to explore this question: what does it say to the life of the Church, to its spirituality and practice, that Christ is specifically known as the 'son of Joseph from Nazareth'?

Perhaps the question might appear quickly settled by stating that ultimately this is an adoptive fatherhood, and Joseph is only the putative father. But that wasn't apparent to the people of Jesus' time. Besides, I enjoy considering that the Messiah of whom Moses and the prophets spoke was seen as the son of Joseph of Nazareth, and lived for 30 years under his instruction. His hands were more a carpenter's than a rabbi's. I like the way John's Gospel weaves together a christology from above, supremely expressed in the prologue, with the so-called christology from below, summarised in Philip's words to Nathanael.

'COME AND SEE'

Philip responds to Nathanael's objection in a fairly pragmatic way: 'Come and see.' Or, to put it another way, take stock yourself of the way things are. This isn't just a hasty attempt to resolve a crucial question, but rather a method that is rooted in the practice of Jesus himself. The invitation Philip extends to Nathanael echoes, in fact, the Master's words to the first two disciples who follow him after the Baptist points him out. To the question 'Rabbi, where are you staying?' Jesus does not reply by giving his address. Instead he replies in an allusive way, with an appeal to interior freedom: one must follow him in order to be welcomed into his home. 'Come and see' is, therefore, at the foundation of the personal journey of seeking and discipleship. Everything begins in this way, by setting out on the journey, accepting that Jesus attracts us because of who he is and not because of what we think of him.

Come and see. Do not stop at your own ideas or preconceived notions. Let the novelty of Jesus surprise you. Become personally aware of the one who comes, who is approaching you. Moses and the prophets spoke of him, and all the scriptures speak of him, but you will not encounter him simply with the scriptures in your hands. He is elusive, mysterious, beyond your interpretation. Come and experience him for yourself. Then you will no longer be scandalised because the Awaited One comes from Nazareth and is the son of Joseph. If you are willing to come and see, you will realise for yourself the indescribable astonishment that the Word of God takes delight in humility, that the Messiah comes from a place you would have expected to produce nothing.

'YOU WILL SEE GREATER THINGS'

Nathanael is an interesting character. He's straightforward and a little blunt. He has no difficulty speaking his mind, but he is also willing to take risks and allow himself to be questioned. Jesus welcomes him with an enthusiasm that shows intimate familiarity, and offers him the chance to realise that Philip hasn't deceived him. In effect, that detail—'while you were under the fig tree, I saw you'—seems to nail Nathanael with the force of the evidence. Only someone who comes from God can display this kind of knowledge! This light dazzles the Israelite in whom there is no duplicity. He feels that Jesus knows everything about him—not only who he is, but also the circumstances: under the fig tree! In the presence of Jesus, he experiences what a good Jew could attribute only to God, as he prayed the words of Psalm 139:

O Lord, you have searched me and known me.
You know when I sit down and when I rise up;
you discern my thoughts from far away.
You search out my path and my lying down,
and are acquainted with all my ways.
Even before a word is on my tongue,
O Lord, you know it completely. (vv. 1–4)

The detail of the fig tree, a decisively eloquent one for Nathanael, remains obscure and mysterious for the reader. The evangelist does not feel obliged to satisfy our curiosity, but instead leaves room for various interpretations. But there is no lack of exegetes who have sought to investigate the meaning of that detail against the background of the scriptures, expressly invoked by Philip (v. 45).

The mention of the fig tree seems to allude to Hosea 9:10: 'Like grapes in the wilderness, I found Israel. Like the first fruit on the fig tree, in its first season, I saw your ancestors.' Against this background, Nathanael would appear to be representative of an Israel faithful to God's promises, unlike the idolatrous generation of which Hosea speaks in the next part of the verse.

The description that Jesus applies to Nathanael, calling him a 'true Israelite' and a man without falsehood, establishes him as a man who has maintained Israel's original authenticity, and has not betrayed his God. Thus, as in the past God chose ancient Israel, now Nathanael, meaning all faithful Israelites, has been chosen by Jesus to be part of his community.[4]

It is a fascinating hypothesis, but, in terms of the narrative, I have no problem with letting the details remain unclear and preserving the aura of mystery surrounding Nathanael's calling. To the one who poked fun at the obscurity of his earthly origin—'Can anything good come from Nazareth?'—Jesus offers a sign of special insight with a vocational message: before Philip called him, Jesus had already 'fixed his eyes on him', and thus had chosen and elected him. As we have seen, in the context of the Last Supper, Jesus will say, 'You did not choose me; on the contrary, I chose you' (John 15:16). This is also true for Nathanael, the guileless Israelite in whom there is no duplicity.

'YOU WILL SEE... THE ANGELS OF GOD ASCENDING AND DESCENDING'

Jesus concludes this dialogue in a solemn manner, with a declaration directed not only to Nathanael but also to the other disciples: 'Amen, amen, I say to you, you will see Heaven opened up and the angels of God ascending and descending upon the Son of Man' (John 1:51).

To Nathanael's surprising experience of 'seeing', Jesus adds another, even fuller, kind of seeing, one as vast as the salvation plan of the Father. The open heavens allude to the possibility of our access to and communion with God's world. This image is reinforced by that of angels ascending and descending on the Son of Man.

We have already noted the reference to Jacob's ladder. But why is the movement of the angels seen first from below to above ('ascending'), before it is depicted from above to below ('descending')? It would seem more logical the other way around. Why do the angels first ascend and then descend the ladder that connects heaven and earth? The answer can be found in the perspective of the prologue. From the moment 'the Word became flesh and dwelt among us', heaven, John seems to be saying, had already descended upon the earth (John 1:14). In effect, the ladder of which Jacob dreams starts from the ground and reaches up to heaven.

In his encyclical *Deus Caritas Est*, Benedict XVI takes up the patristic interpretation of this image:

In the account of Jacob's ladder, the Fathers of the Church saw this inseparable connection between ascending and descending love, between eros which seeks God and agape which passes on the gift received, symbolised in various ways. In that biblical passage we read how the Patriarch Jacob saw in a dream, above the stone which was his pillow, a ladder reaching up to heaven, on which the angels of God were ascending and descending (cf. Genesis 28:12; John 1:51). A particularly striking interpretation of this vision is presented by Pope Gregory the Great in his Pastoral Rule. He tells us that the good pastor must be rooted in contemplation. Only in this way will he be able to take upon himself the needs of others and make them his own... Saint Gregory speaks in this context of Saint Paul, who was borne aloft to the most exalted mysteries of God, and hence, having descended once more, was able to become all things to all men (cf. 2 Corinthians 12:2–4; 1 Corinthians 9:22).[5]

In order to see the heavens opened, we must follow Jesus—but not as Philip and Nathanael were probably expecting. The Son of Man completes his ascension into heaven by following to the very end the way of love, a disarmed and disarming love that forgives and gives of itself to the point of allowing one's heart to be torn open. And, like heaven, this wound will remain open for ever.

DIALOGUING WITH THE WORD

What an experience it is to meet Jesus! Andrew and the other disciple, whose name is not mentioned, never forget how they encountered him... To meet Jesus is to have a direct experience of love; it is to feel accepted, understood, forgiven.

 Look back over your life. Do you remember a moment when you felt Jesus' eyes turned upon you? How do you remember that moment? How do you treasure it? Let yourself be fixed again by the penetrating gaze of the one who loves you and invites you to follow him.

How is it possible to conceal this love? To meet Jesus means letting yourself be overtaken by his self-giving. He came as the divine presence of love, as the Lamb who takes away the sin of the world, as the liberating Messiah. He is the ladder of Jacob's dream, the ladder that places heaven and earth in communication. Through Jesus, you too can ascend to heaven and rest in the bosom of God.

Meeting Jesus means learning a new way of being; it means becoming an expert in communication. This occurs not through learning new techniques and strategies, but because Love propels us from within; it wants to be communicated. Thus Andrew runs to Simon, and Philip to Nathanael. Communication happens through different words, in a more concise or lengthy form, but with a single message and the same goal: to bring our brother or friend to Jesus. How do you live out the communicative and missionary dimension of the faith? Do you feel the urgency and joy of communicating Jesus to all who seek him, to the brothers and sisters who do not think about him or think they are far from him?

✛

PAUSE TO PONDER

'Before Philip called you...'
Lord, you continue to call us through others,
reaching us through the invitation of a friend;
you always love us concretely
through someone else.

But it is always YOU.
Yours is the gaze that wounds the heart.
You reach out to us beneath our fig tree or our apple tree,
and wake us, like the beloved in the Song of Songs.[6]
You rouse us from our drowsiness,
from our preconceptions and certainties,
and you set us on the journey.
You are the Awaited One who comes
in ways we did not imagine.
Yes, even from Nazareth,
the humble village of Galilee,
you come not with the soft hands of a rabbi,
but with the calloused hands
of the son of Joseph, the craftsman.
You know life's hardships
and understand perfectly the human heart.
You search me, and you know me.
You see my sincerity and my desire to meet you.
You see my dreams and my fleeting enthusiasms,
you see my hopes and my unavoidable disappointments,
and you call me.
You call me through someone like Philip,
but in reality you have called me before this,
from all eternity.
Even before you created the world, you chose me to be holy and
spotless in love.
You came down from heaven to take me back with you.
You are more than a ladder,
you are the elevator that carries me straight up
in the most tender embrace of the Father.
I want to follow you with complete trust
in your word that promises to me, too,
the vision of greater things,
the vision of your glory.

Chapter 3

THE MOTHER OF JESUS AND WINE FOR THE WEDDING

While the Synoptic Gospels do not mention Cana, this location plays an important role in John's Gospel. Jesus works his first miracle or 'sign' there. Cana also constitutes the point of departure and return for a journey that is simultaneously narrative, geographic and symbolic. This journey frames Jesus' gradual revelation: from Cana to Galilee to Jerusalem, and then, through Samaria, back to Cana. Thus John 2:1—4:54 forms an important section that we could call 'from Cana to Cana'.

FROM CANA TO CANA: THE JOURNEY OF REVELATION AND FAITH

In the way this journey unfolds, we can detect the gradual emergence of faith in Jesus: from the first disciples, to the believers in Jerusalem, to the women and people of Samaria, and even to the pagans, represented by the royal official and his family:

- In Cana of Galilee, Jesus manifests his glory, and 'his disciples believed in him' (John 2:11), becoming the first to do so.
- In Jerusalem, during the Passover feast, 'many believed in his name' (John 2:23) after seeing the miraculous signs that he worked.

- In Sychar, through the witness borne by the Samaritan woman, and then through the people's own direct experience, many 'Samaritans... believed based upon his word' (John 4:4–42).
- Back in Cana, Jesus heals the son of the royal official, the first fruit of the pagans: 'he believed, along with his whole household' (John 4:46–54).

We should note that the evangelist constructs a careful parallelism between the two signs/miracles of Cana. These present the same literary structure and share the thematic concern regarding true faith:

First sign at Cana: John 2:1–11	Second sign at Cana: John 4:46–54
1. Problem: The wine fails (v. 3).	1. Problem: An official's son is ill (v. 46).
2. Request: The mother of Jesus says to him, 'They have no wine' (v. 3).	2. Request: The official comes to Jesus and begs him to come and heal his son (v. 47).
3. Rebuke: 'What do you want from me, woman?' (v. 4).	3. Rebuke: 'Unless you see signs and wonders you do not believe!' (v. 48)
4. Reaction: His mother says to the servants, 'Do whatever he tells (Greek: *legein*) you' (v. 5).	4. Reaction: 'Go your way, your son will live.' The man believes the word (Greek: *lógos*) that Jesus speaks to him (v. 50).
5. Consequence: A miracle that leads to the faith of others (disciples) (vv. 6–11).	5. Consequence: A miracle that leads to the faith of others (household) (vv. 51–53).

Both scenes are rounded off with a comment from the evangelist, showing that he is anxious for his reader to notice that these two accounts of miracles performed at Cana are a statement and a restatement of the same themes.[1]

2:11 Jesus did this, the first of his signs, at Cana in Galilee.	4:54 Jesus did this second sign as he was coming from Judea into Galilee.

The distinct parallelism between these two signs marks a clear narrative grouping, meaning that the section from 2:1 to 4:54 must be taken as a whole. In effect, along the journey from Cana to Cana, the evangelist gradually reveals the glory of Jesus, who is the true temple, the only-begotten Son of the Father, the Saviour of the world. This section also marks a progressive arrival at faith: from the first nucleus of believers at Cana of Galilee to an increasingly broader circle of people from Jerusalem, Samaria, and even from among the pagans, as represented by the royal official. In Cana, as the servants did at the urging of Mary, the official obeys the word of Jesus.

THE NUPTIAL CONTEXT OF THE FIRST SIGN

The traditional site of Cana is Kefr Kenna, six miles north-east of Nazareth. John's account reflects the joyous atmosphere of a wedding feast:

On the third day there was a wedding in Cana of Galilee, and Jesus' mother was there.

Now Jesus and his disciples had also been invited to the wedding, and when the wine ran out Jesus' mother said to him, 'They have no wine.'

Jesus replied, 'What do you want from me, woman? My hour has not come yet.'

His mother said to the servants, 'Do whatever he tells you.'

Now six stone water jars were standing there, in accordance with the Jewish purification rites, each holding twenty to thirty gallons.

Jesus said to them, 'Fill the water jars with water.' And they filled them to the brim.

Then he said to them, 'Now draw some out and take it to the head steward.' So they took it.

When the head steward tasted the water which had become wine—and he did not know where it came from, while the servants who had drawn the water did know—the head steward called the bridegroom and said to him, 'Every man first puts out the good wine, then when they are drunk he puts out the lesser wine; *you have* kept the good wine till *now*!'

Jesus did this, the first of his signs, at Cana in Galilee and revealed his glory, and his disciples believed in him. (John 2:1–11)[2]

The evangelist introduces the narrative with an indication of time: 'On the third day'. The third day is the preferred time for great signs, and alludes to the resurrection (see John 2:19; 4:43; 11:6).

'*Jesus' mother was there.*' Mary is the first person to be presented. She is decisive in the development of this passage, as she will be again at the foot of the cross. But John never calls her by name. He refers to her as Jesus' mother (2:12; 19:25). In Jesus' culture, calling a woman 'the mother of' someone was an honorary title.

'*Jesus and his disciples had also been invited to the wedding.*' Jesus has by now formed a stable group with his disciples, and they are invited to the wedding together. In reality, the disciples are the intended audience of the miraculous sign that reveals the messianic identity of Jesus.

The account unfolds in four scenes:

- The initiative of Jesus' mother (John 2:3–5)
- Jesus and the servants (vv. 6–8)
- The admiration of the head steward (vv. 9–10)
- The conclusion (v. 11)

JESUS' MOTHER ANTICIPATES HIS HOUR

In the Greek text, Mary speaks a total of nine words: three of these are addressed to her son, and six to the servants. To Jesus, his mother simply says, '*óinon oúk échousin*' ('They have no wine'). But in these three words, she says everything. They express first her attentiveness to what was happening around her; then her desire to help, to find a fitting and dignified solution to the problem; and lastly her certainty that her Son can provide this help. She knows very well to whom she should turn.

This passage clearly shows the twofold level of meaning characteristic of the fourth Gospel, which moves easily from the literal to the symbolic. Wine has a strong symbolic resonance in the Old Testament, especially in connection with a wedding banquet. In the Prophets, it is a sign of salvation and of the magnificence of the messianic era (Amos 9:13–14; Isaiah 25:6; Joel 2:24).

How does Jesus react to his mother's request? One might say that he responds coldly: he seems evasive, distant. And he replies with a question: 'What do you want from me, woman?' This sounds harsh to our ears, even if, as the experts say, the original expression is a colloquial phrase whose precise meaning depends on the context. 'It seems that Jesus wants to clarify his position and that of his mother in relation to the twofold meaning that wine expresses. Mary is preoccupied with the material wine for the wedding; Jesus has in mind the symbolic wine of the messianic era.'[3] This wine is strictly connected with his 'hour', meaning the Paschal mystery, the hour of Jesus' passion and glorification.

How does Mary react? She does not act offended, she does not reply to her son's question, and she is not concerned about clarifying the meaning or tone of his words. Instead, with great calmness and confidence she turns to the servants and says, 'Do whatever he tells you' (*hó ti àn lége humín poiesate*). This phrase echoes the words of Pharaoh when he sends the Egyptians to Joseph at the beginning of the seven years of famine. He instructs them to do whatever Joseph tells them (Genesis 41:55). But apart from its literary background, John's Gospel clearly displays Mary's function as a mediator. She presents the need—the lack of wine—to her son, and teaches us the proper attitude towards him: 'Do whatever he tells you.'

'*Now six stone water jars were standing there, in accordance with the Jewish purification rites.*' Why six? This number does not seem accidental. Nothing is added by mere chance to the fourth Gospel. Every detail is carefully chosen according to a precise meaning, even if the meaning is sometimes symbolic and elusive. In this case, biblical commentators are inclined to link the 'six jars' with the 'six days' of creation (see Genesis 1:3—2:2). In continuity with Jewish tradition, ancient Christian thought attributes prophetic significance to the account of creation in Genesis: the six days of creation symbolise the six ages of the world, or the six millennia in which God brings the work of his hands to perfection. Before him, in fact, a thousand years are as one day (Psalm 90:4). 'The sixth day, on which God created man, is a prophecy of the sixth day on which he will recreate it, in Christ, at the end of time.'[4]

'*And they filled them to the brim.*' Obedient to the word of Jesus, according to the directions his mother gave them, the servants fill the six jars to the brim. Then comes the transformation. And what surprise and wonder—the wine is extraordinarily good! The first one astounded by this is the expert, the 'head steward', who tells the bridegroom, 'Every man first puts out the good wine, then when they are drunk he puts out the lesser wine; you have kept the good wine till now!' (John 2:10).

A TRANSFORMATION THAT RECALLS OTHERS

The transformation of water into wine is situated within a broad symbolic landscape that plays on three elements: water, wine, Spirit. The first two elements refer symbolically to the third, the Spirit whom Jesus gives, and who has the power to make us be 'born again, from above' (John 3:5).

- In Egypt, the water becomes blood (first plague): an ambivalent sign that strengthens the faith of the Israelites and calls upon the Egyptians to acknowledge the divine law.
- At Cana, the water becomes wine: the first sign that manifests Jesus' messianic identity and his power to give the Spirit, symbolised by the wine.
- In the upper room, the wine becomes blood: this is the supreme sign pointing to Jesus' sacrifice and the new creation that is realised on the cross, in the symbols of water, blood and Spirit.

The third transformation, from wine to blood, combines the end-points of the two previous transformations. In order to liberate his people from slavery, God changes water into blood. For the joy of the wedding feast, Jesus transforms water into wine. And to seal the definitive covenant, the eternal wedding feast, he transforms wine into his blood.

DIALOGUING WITH THE WORD

At Cana of Galilee, Jesus' mother anticipates his hour and plays a part in revealing his identity. Her disclosure agrees with that of the Baptist in the following chapter: Jesus is the Messiah, the one who 'gives the Spirit without measure' (John 3:34). He is the authentic Bridegroom, for whom all creation yearns.

The wine that Jesus offers at Cana, in addition to being exquisite, is superabundant: six jars filled to the brim (about 150 gallons!). Jesus is not satisfied with what is strictly necessary. He came that we might 'have life and have it abundantly' (John 10:10). Are you open to this superabundance, or do you limit yourself to what is strictly necessary?

Is there anything the son can deny his mother? She alone can place herself so boldly into God's realm of boundless generosity. Here Mary does not ask health for the sick, or plead for some seemingly great cause, but simply to ensure that the wine will not run out, and with it the singing and dancing. The mother of Jesus enters the scene so that the wedding feast may continue.

At Cana, Mary thus reveals not only Jesus but also herself. She distinguishes herself as a woman aware of the situation, but also aware of Jesus' power. She holds the compass in her hands, so to speak: she is good at orienting herself; she knows immediately to whom she must go to resolve the problem. And she teaches us the right attitude towards Jesus, an attitude of obedient listening.

What sort of wine risks running dry in our families and church communities? Let us pray for the formative journey of engaged and married couples and pray that there will be no lack of the symbolic wine of listening, understanding and openness to the will of God. Mary always leads us to Jesus. Today, too, she invites each one of us with the same words she addressed to the servants in Cana: 'Do whatever he tells you.'

PAUSE TO PONDER

Holy Mary of the wedding at Cana,
watchful and discreet woman
on the side of those who serve for the joy of the feast,
you are the first to realise that the wine is gone,
and with a few direct words
you call upon Jesus without hesitation.
You are the Mother of Revelation.
Bring about the future hour,
the hour of the new and excellent wine,
the gift of the Bridegroom.
Holy Mary of the wedding at Cana,
you reveal the glory of Christ,
who is in solidarity with the joy
of every man and woman at the wedding feast.
You who know the path of life,
teach us the art of prolonging the feast
by doing, like the servants at Cana,
everything that he tells us.

✳

Chapter 4

THE NIGHT-TIME CONVERSATION BETWEEN JESUS AND NICODEMUS

I can see again, in my mind's eye, the little houses of the Jewish neighbourhood of Mea Shearim, shrouded in the silence of the evening hour of prayer. I lived near there while studying in Jerusalem. When I walked through the crowded streets of that neighbourhood, I was struck by the glow from the houses that showed, against the curtains, the shadows of men hunched over their sacred books, wrapped in the mantle of prayer: 'I commune with my heart in the night; I meditate and search my spirit' (Psalm 77:6). Nicodemus was a seeker in the night. Jesus' first discourse in the Gospel of John is dedicated to Nicodemus. It is an unforgettable dialogue, the warmth of a light in the darkness.

IN THE NIGHT

The mysterious Nicodemus comes furtively on to the stage, as if on tiptoe. This Pharisee and leader of the Jews expresses admiration for the rabbi of Nazareth, and perhaps something more: 'Rabbi, we know that you are a teacher come from God, because no one can do the signs you are doing unless God is with him' (John 3:2).

Nicodemus speaks in the plural: 'we know'. Whom does he represent? He stands for the secret sympathisers who were present even among the Pharisees and other Jewish leaders. During their conversation, Jesus describes him as a 'teacher of Israel'. Nicodemus was probably a Pharisaic scribe of the Sanhedrin, the highest body of autonomous Jewish administration under the Roman occupation. Nicodemus comes to honour Jesus in his own name, but also in the name of his colleagues. They observed Jesus during the pilgrimage for the feast of *Pesach* (the Jewish Passover). They recognised the action of God in the signs that he performed, especially the cleansing of the temple. Seized by zeal for the house of his Father, Jesus drove out from the temple those who sold oxen, sheep and doves, overturning the moneychangers' tables (John 2:13–16). Nicodemus probably witnessed this scene and asked himself, 'Who is this rabbi?'

The evangelist notes, 'Now while he was in Jerusalem for the Passover, at the festival, many believed in his name when they saw the signs he was doing' (John 2:23). Not yet a true believer, Nicodemus is asking questions. He is honestly seeking the truth; the person of Jesus catches his curiosity and he cannot sleep. Drawn powerfully by the light, Nicodemus overcomes his night-time drowsiness and goes to see Jesus. Let us follow him as well.

THE STRUCTURE OF JOHN 3:1–21

- This passage is marked off by the change of time and place in 3:22. The first two verses of chapter 3 introduce the scene and present Nicodemus, who is the first to speak: 'Rabbi, we know…' (v. 2).
- In verse 3, Jesus replies as a true 'teacher', introducing the theme that characterises his entire discourse: 'Amen, amen, I say to you, unless you are born from above, you cannot see the Kingdom of God.'
- Verse 4 contains the objection of Nicodemus, formulated as a pair of questions: 'How can a man be born when he is old?

Surely he cannot go into his mother's womb and be born a second time?'

- In verses 5–8, Jesus takes up again the theme of birth from above, clarifying and amplifying it. His reply is introduced in the same way: 'Amen, amen, I say to you, if you are not born of water and the Spirit you cannot enter the Kingdom of God.'

- In verse 9, Nicodemus asks, 'How can these things be?'

- Jesus replies with another question, which addresses Nicodemus in his capacity as a teacher and reveals that even he truly does not know: 'You are a teacher of Israel and do not know these things?' (v. 10).

- There follows the third 'Amen, amen, I say to you,' and a reversal of the situation: now it is Jesus who speaks in the plural and asserts his authentic knowledge: 'We speak of what we know, and we bear witness to what we've seen, yet you don't accept our witness' (v. 11). This 'we/you' format continues at verse 12, and indicates an expansion of the context to the discussions between Christians and Jews at the time of the evangelist. In other words, this account is emblematic of the community situation: in speaking to Nicodemus, Jesus is addressing the Jews who are willing to enter into dialogue, and becomes himself the spokesman of the Church's faith.

- The question of Nicodemus is answered in verses 13–21, but Nicodemus seems already to have left the scene. He disappears without his departure being mentioned—but why? We will understand better as we continue to explore the text, but we should note at this point that Nicodemus will be contrasted with the Samaritan woman with whom Jesus speaks in the following chapter. She remains present until the conclusion of the scene and becomes a witness to Jesus. But this is not what Nicodemus does in his night-time conversation.[1]

- This passage ends, significantly, with a contrast between light and darkness. The supreme revelation of God's love for the world

(v. 16) implies the *krísis*, or verdict, that is involved: 'The light came into the world, yet men loved the darkness rather than the light' (v. 19). This echoes a fundamental theme, anticipated in the prologue (John 1:5, 9–10).

BEING BORN OF WATER AND THE SPIRIT

In a veiled manner at first, and then more explicitly and directly, Jesus examines a subject that must have been familiar to Nicodemus, a 'teacher of Israel'—being born from the Spirit.

Like the disciples of Jesus, Nicodemus addresses him as 'Rabbi' and acknowledges that he is 'a teacher come from God' (v. 2). This matter is of the greatest importance, because in his Gospel John repeatedly tells us that Jesus comes from God, and only from God. If Nicodemus actually believes what he is saying, he should behave differently. That is what John expects from those who read and hear his Gospel.

After Nicodemus greets and honours him, Jesus begins to speak without having been asked any direct question. He is the one who chooses the topic of conversation, and he introduces it in a solemn manner, with the formula of the double 'amen' that confers the greatest significance on his remarks: 'Amen, amen, I say to you, no one can see the kingdom of God without being born from above' (v. 3).

This is the first time that John's Gospel uses the expression *'basiléia toú Theoú'*, 'kingdom of God', which occurs so frequently in the synoptic Gospels. Outside of this discourse, in which it appears twice, we will not find it again.[2] And yet it appears at the opening of the discussion, which undoubtedly points to its importance. '[Seeing] the kingdom of God' objectively corresponds to '[entering] the kingdom of God' and signifies taking part in it, becoming personally involved in it.

Two texts from the synoptic Gospels are fairly close to this assertion about the need to be born again in order to see/enter the kingdom. The first is Mark 10:15: 'Amen, I say to you, whoever doesn't accept the Kingdom of God like a child shall not enter it!' The other is Matthew 18:3: 'Amen, I say to you, Unless you turn about and become like children, you will not ever enter the Kingdom of Heaven!' John speaks more radically of a birth. This is not a matter of simply becoming 'like' children (there is no such comparative word in our text!) but of receiving, through rebirth, a new origin. One's origin is something that is received, not acquired.

Nicodemus does not understand Jesus' affirmation. Actually, the term *ánothen*, which the evangelist uses in verse 3, lends itself to misinterpretation because it has two possible meanings: 'from above' and 'again'. Nicodemus settles on the second meaning and objects, 'How can a man... be born a second time?'

But his question allows the discourse to move forward. Jesus does not humiliate Nicodemus but continues his explanation, expanding and deepening it. Now it becomes clear that in Jesus' statement *ánothen* indicates both meanings: 'again' and 'from above'.

Being born again 'from above' (v. 3) corresponds to 'being born of water and the Spirit' (v. 5). A 'teacher' like Nicodemus should know this. In effect, this is what the Scriptures proclaim, in particular the prophets Jeremiah and Ezekiel. In exile, Israel is promised a time when God will sprinkle him with pure water, and place within him his own spirit.

'I will sprinkle clean water upon you, and you shall be clean from all your uncleannesses, and from all your idols I will cleanse you. A new heart I will give you, and a new spirit I will put within you; and I will remove from your body the heart of stone and give you a heart of flesh. I will put my spirit within you, and make you follow my statutes and be careful to observe my ordinances.' (Ezekiel 36:25–27)

Only the Spirit (v. 8) brings about the 'new' birth, the birth 'from above'. In John, as in the Jewish tradition, 'from above' means 'from heaven'. The new birth is the gift of an origin that is not earthly but heavenly, like that of Jesus, who is 'from above' (John 8:23). Being born of the Spirit means receiving from God a new beginning, which frees us from the burden of our former life. Yes, it is possible to be born again, even when we are old!

Along with the Spirit, verse 5 mentions water. Rudolf Schnackenburg comments, 'Any Christian hearing or reading the Gospel must have thought of baptism immediately.'[3] And in his book *Jesus of Nazareth*, Benedict XVI writes:

Rebirth—to put it another way—involves the creative power of God's Spirit, but it also requires the sacrament of the maternal womb of the receiving and welcoming Church. Photina Rech cites Tertullian: Never was Christ without water (Tertullian, De baptismo, IX, 4). She then gives this somewhat enigmatic saying of the early Church writer its correct interpretation: 'Christ never was, and never is, without the Ekklesia' (Rech, Inbild, II, p. 304). Spirit and water, heaven and earth, Christ and the Church, belong together. And that is how 'rebirth' happens. In the sacrament, water stands for the maternal earth, the holy Church, which welcomes creation into herself and stands in place of it.[4]

But let's continue reading the text. Nicodemus asks how all of this could be possible (John 3:9). Jesus gives a long reply that can be divided into three parts:

- Verses 10–13: Jesus speaks to the 'teacher of Israel' as someone who truly understands and knows, a witness who tells what he has seen: he can speak of the birth from above because he himself comes from above.
- Verses 14–17: This central part presents, so to speak, the heart of this rebirth. What truly makes this possible is God's love for the world, which he manifests through the gift of his Son: 'So

that everyone who believes in him will not die but will have eternal life' (v. 16).

- Verses 18–21: The third part, finally, deals with the consequences resulting from God's love for the world. It is always a challenge for us to convey together both of God's main attributes: justice and mercy. But this passage embraces both of these, demonstrating the world's reaction to the love of God, or the contrast between believers and nonbelievers. Here resistance to the light is not prompted by ideological factors; rather, it is practical, behavioural: '... everyone who does evil hates the light, and does not come into the light lest his works be made known' (v. 20). In contrast, '... whoever does the truth comes to the light so his works may be revealed as wrought in God' (v. 21).

How does Nicodemus react? We have already noted that Nicodemus has asked all of his questions by verse 9. He doesn't reply to Jesus' question in verse 10, nor does he react to the long discourse that follows. He simply disappears from the scene, with no notification to the reader. When does he return?

The evangelist mentions him two other times in the course of his account. We find him again in Jerusalem, in the context of the Feast of Booths (*Sukkot*), and then in the dramatic aftermath of the death and burial of Jesus.

Disturbed by Jesus' success, the high priests and Pharisees send guards to arrest him in the middle of the feast of *Sukkot* (John 7: 32–36). But they return at the end of the feast without having done anything, exclaiming, 'Never did a man speak like that!' (v. 46). Their admiration hardens the opposition to Jesus. The Pharisees, who appear as a fairly powerful group in the Gospel of John, insult the people as ignorant; only gullible people would follow Jesus, believing him to be the Christ.

But Nicodemus objects to their judgment. The evangelist reminds the reader who he is: 'the one who had come to Jesus previously, he was one of them' (John 7:50). Nicodemus disagrees with his colleagues' behaviour, trying to persuade them to act in keeping with the Jewish law. But he fails in his aim, and instead raises suspicion that he is among the Nazarene's sympathisers (v. 52). From this point on, he is silent.

He returns after the crucifixion. He appears together with Joseph of Arimathea, described as 'a disciple of Jesus, but a secret one' (John 19:38). Both are among the 'leaders' who, out of fear of being expelled from the synagogue, dare not confess their faith (12:43). John certainly does not praise these men, but instead comments, '... they loved the glory of men more than the glory of God'. This is Nicodemus' problem. Not so with Paul, a converted Pharisee, who can say, 'If I were still trying to please men, I wouldn't be a servant of Christ!' (Galatians 1:10).

Nevertheless, the final appearance of this man who went at night to talk to Jesus cannot help but arouse admiration in the Christian community. 'Nicodemus came, too—the one who had first come to him at night—bringing a mixture of myrrh and aloes, about a hundred pounds' (John 19:39). While before he had refused to take a clear position, limiting himself to disapproving of his colleagues' fanaticism, he now acts decisively, revealing 'the possibility of acting humanely, something that not everyone in that kind of situation is able to do'.[5] Thus Nicodemus seems, at last, to emerge from the night and come into the light in this preparation for Passover.

DIALOGUING WITH THE WORD

Enter into the silence of your heart. Invoke the gift of the Holy Spirit. Listen deeply to the instruction of the 'Master come from God'. The Spirit is like the wind. The evangelist plays on the double meaning of the Greek term *pneúma*, which, like the Hebrew word *ruach*, indicates both 'wind' and 'spirit'. The wind/spirit blows where it will. Its action is sovereign; it cannot be captured. Are you able to recognise in yourself, in others, in history, the voice of the wind/spirit?

Are you aware of the new life that was given to you in baptism? How do you cultivate it? 'What is born of flesh is flesh,' Jesus says, 'and what is born of spirit is spirit.' Being born of the Spirit implies, by its nature, acting according to that same Spirit (see Romans 8). Just as it is possible to hear the voice of the wind/spirit, so also it should be possible to perceive (even on the part of those who do not believe) the spiritual vitality of those who are born of the Spirit.

'We speak of what we know, and we bear witness to what we have seen,' Jesus declares to Nicodemus. John, in turn, speaks of what he knows through direct experience; he testifies to what he has seen and contemplated (1 John 1:1–3). Woe to us if we speak of what we do not know! Yet a purely intellectual knowledge would be insufficient. We are called to bear witness to what we ourselves have experienced through faith and the sacramental life. What is our experience of Jesus?

Thank the heavenly Father for his immense love. Saint Irenaeus writes:

The glory of God gives life; those who see God receive life. For this reason God, who cannot be grasped, comprehended, or seen, allows himself to be seen, comprehended, and grasped by men, that he may give life to those who see and receive him. It is impossible to live without life, and the actualisation of life comes from participation in God, while participation in God is to see God and enjoy his goodness. Men will therefore see God if they are to live; through the vision of God they will become immortal and attain to God himself. As I have said, this was shown in symbols by the prophets: God will be seen by men who bear his Spirit and are always waiting for his coming... Life in man is the glory of God; the life of man is the vision of God. If the revelation of God through creation gives life to all who live upon the earth, much more does the manifestation of the Father through the Word give life to those who see God. (From the Treatise Against Heresies)

✛

PAUSE TO PONDER

You, Nicodemus, are the witness to an unforgettable encounter
in the night.
How grateful we are to you, 'teacher of Israel', for your visit to the
'Teacher come from God'!
But tell us, what did you take away from that encounter?
Why did you stop asking questions?
His words must have seemed so senseless to you.
Is it really possible to be born again? And how?
How can we be freed from the burdens of our past,
how can we escape our faults?
'Create in me a clean heart, O God,
and put a new and right spirit within me.
Do not cast me away from your presence,
and do not take your holy spirit from me' (Psalm 51:10–11).
As a good Pharisee, you, Nicodemus, are too concerned about
what man must do.
And yet, you who are a teacher
must know the great hope that dwells within Israel:
not only an old man, but even a pile of dry bones can be reborn,
when the Spirit blows (see Ezekiel 37).
Behold, the time has come;
it has been granted you to be reborn
in order to enter the kingdom.

Behold, God so loved the world that he gave his Son.
You did not understand all this that night,
but from that moment on you did not stop searching.
And on the last night you arrived
with a great abundance of perfume,
the prelude to Easter rebirth.

※

Chapter 5

JESUS AT THE WELL WITH THE SAMARITAN WOMAN

In the Bible, encounters that take place at wells follow a narrative formula with common features and usually conclude with a marriage, according to this outline:

- A man travels to a foreign land.
- He finds a well.
- A woman arrives (or several women: see Exodus 2:16).
- A conversation occurs about the water that is given.
- A conversation follows about the man's identity.
- The woman runs home to spread the news.
- The foreigner is invited to the home; a meal and wedding follow.

The servant of Abraham, sent by the patriarch to the land of his birth in order to choose a wife for his son Isaac, meets the splendid Rebecca at a well (Genesis 24:10–51). Jacob meets his beautiful shepherd girl, Rachel, at a well (Genesis 29:9–14), and Moses meets his future wife at a well (Exodus 2:15–22).

Naturally each account has its variations, and, in the case of the story of the Samaritan woman, the variation of the formula comes at the end. But why did the evangelist John tell us of the meeting between Jesus and the Samaritan woman at a well, knowing the reader's expectation for the story's ending? What is he trying to tell us? This question can help us to read the text again from a new perspective: the journey of faith leads us to recognise Jesus as

Messiah/Bridegroom. The Baptist vouches for this, '[rejoicing] with joy at the bridegroom's voice' (John 3:29).

The messianic time is the time of the wedding, the time of fidelity to the marital alliance, the time in which the true worshippers 'will worship the Father in spirit and truth' (John 4:23).

AT THE WELL OF SYCHAR

The beginning of chapter 4 shows Jesus returning from Jerusalem to Galilee: 'he left Judea and went off to Galilee again' (v. 3). Instead of going back along the Jordan River, or by way of the Via Maris that winds along the shores of the Mediterranean, he chooses the more difficult path, which passes through the mountains of Samaria. It is about midday when he arrives at the gates of Shechem. His disciples go to buy something to eat (v. 8). Worn out by the journey, Jesus sits beside the well that tradition attributed to the patriarch Jacob.

And now a woman comes 'to draw water' (v. 7). Why would she go to the well at the hottest time of day? Typically people remained indoors at midday to eat and rest. We know that women usually went to draw water from the well in the evening (see Genesis 24:11), at the end of the day, when it was cooler and they could take a moment to relax and chat with friends.

Why, then, would the Samaritan woman go to draw water at the hottest hour of the day? Perhaps it was simply in the hope of not meeting anyone, of being able to draw water quickly and return home undisturbed. Her personal situation must have been known openly in the small town, and she was probably the butt of jokes and gossip when women gathered at the well.

Here she is at the well now, and a man, a stranger, is there. She doesn't say a word to him, but he immediately addresses a request to her: 'Give me a drink.' With subtle artistry, the evangelist John thus begins one of the most beautiful dialogues in his Gospel. Jesus takes the initiative: he engages the woman. But at a certain point she takes charge and directs the conversation. In the end, Jesus is the one being questioned. It is to this woman—and only to her—that he expressly reveals himself as the Messiah.

'IF YOU KNEW THE GIFT OF GOD!'

At first, the woman keeps her distance. The stranger's request appears to go against social norms: 'How is it that you, a Jew, ask me, a Samaritan woman, for a drink?' The evangelist notes that relations between Jews and Samaritans were not good for both political and religious reasons. The Samaritans had built a temple on Mount Gerizim and maintained that this was the legitimate place of worship. The Jews believed that the Samaritans were half-pagan and idolaters. The woman is therefore astonished that a Jew would speak to her and even ask her for something.

How does Jesus react? He does not offer socio-political explanations: instead he puts into doubt her initial assessment. She had just referred to him as 'a Jew', but he advances a reservation: 'If you knew the gift of God and who it is who is saying to you, "Give me a drink"...'

So she doesn't know who he is. She does not know the gift of God that stands before her. If she had known, she would have been the one asking him for water. The woman's curiosity is aroused, and she listens: gift of God, living water. What a strange way of reasoning this stranger has—completely impractical: 'Lord, you have no bucket and the well is deep, so where do you get the living water from? Surely you are not greater than our father Jacob.'

Jesus doesn't explain what he means by 'gift' and 'living water'. He continues to speak enigmatically: 'Everyone who drinks this water will thirst again. But whoever drinks the water I will give him will never thirst.' The woman reacts immediately: 'Lord, give me this water so I will not become thirsty.' Jesus has hit his mark.

'GO CALL YOUR HUSBAND': THE EXISTENTIAL TRUTH

The dialogue now takes a new direction. The Master makes another request: 'Go and call your husband and come here.' Poor woman! She had come out at midday to avoid the sly smiles, the whispered comments, the rumours, and here is a stranger who brings up the crucial point. 'I do not have a husband,' she quickly replies. He shoots back, 'You were right when you said, "I do not have a husband"—you have had five men and the one you have now isn't your husband.'

It should be noted that she is not offended by this. Instead, the knowledge of her life that Jesus demonstrates opens her eyes to his mysterious identity: 'Lord, I see that you are a prophet.'

It might seem that the woman is shrewdly changing the subject, but this is not a clever attempt to start a theology discussion in order to avoid shedding light on her own life. Jesus has shown that he knows her story in an intimate way, possible only for God, or for a man of God such as a prophet. Therefore the woman recognises Jesus as a prophet. And as such, he has much more to reveal to her.

FROM HER TRUTH TO HIS TRUTH

This dynamic narrative unfolds clearly from what follows. Jesus does not reprimand the woman for changing the subject and evading his request. Instead, he responds to her in the same vein, moving to a more explicit revelation: 'Believe me, woman, the hour is coming when you will worship the Father neither on this mountain nor in Jerusalem... God is Spirit, and those who worship Him must worship in Spirit and truth' (vv. 21–24). The woman replies: 'I know that the Messiah is coming.' At this point, Jesus uncovers his true identity: 'I who am speaking to you am he.'

The scene then becomes more animated with the arrival of the disciples, who are astonished to find Jesus speaking with a woman.

However, they hold back from questioning him. The Samaritan woman leaves in a hurry, even leaving her water jar behind. She has already drunk the living water that Jesus had promised her, and she has no time to waste. The news that she has is too wonderful, and she has to communicate it. She runs to the town feeling very free.

She no longer has to hide from her past. She's not afraid of the looks of disapproval from people or their remarks. Enthusiastically, she recounts her own experience. What had only the day before been a source of humiliation and shame can now be recounted freely. Moreover, it becomes the very basis of her witness and proclamation: 'Come see a man who told me everything I've done! Could this be the Messiah?' (v. 29).

BEYOND THE NARRATIVE FORMULA: THE SAMARITAN WOMAN AND HER PEOPLE

While encounters at a well usually end with a wedding, in this case there is none! How should this surprising conclusion be interpreted? On the historical level, the answer is obvious: Jesus never married. But what about the symbolic level? Why does the evangelist John present the meeting between Jesus and the Samaritan woman at a well, knowing what this would evoke in the reader's mind?

John seems to enjoy playing with double meanings. He has already done this by speaking of 'living' water. The woman may have thought of this water as nothing more than a fresh spring, but on the lips of Jesus the term recalls the Spirit. Here, playing with the narrative formula, John has also begun the story with a surprise variation to the theme. The Samaritan woman is not even a marriageable young woman, as had been Rebecca or Rachel or the daughters of Reuel (whom Moses meets in Exodus 2). Indeed, her problem is not finding a husband: she's already had five. Her problem is finding her true husband.

She represents her people, the Samaritans. They were considered heretics and infidels by the Jews. They had abandoned the God of Israel, their 'only true husband'.

St Augustine sees in this woman a figure of the Church formed from the pagans:

In that woman, then, let us hear ourselves, and in her acknowledge ourselves, and in her give our own thanks to God. For she was the symbol, not the reality; for she both first showed forth the figure and became the reality. For she believed in him who set her forth as a symbol to teach us. She came then to draw water. She had simply come to draw water; as people are accustomed to do...

The woman brought a vessel for drawing water. She was surprised that a Jew asked her for a drink—something that the Jews would not usually do. But he who was asking for a drink was thirsting for the faith of the woman herself...

He asks for a drink, and he promises to give a drink. He longs for it as one about to receive; he abounds as one about to satisfy others' thirst. He says: 'If you knew the gift of God.' The gift of God is the Holy Spirit. But he still speaks to the woman guardedly, and enters into her heart by degrees. It may be he is now teaching her. For what could be sweeter and kinder than that exhortation? 'If you knew the gift of God.' So far he has kept her in suspense...

What water will he give, except that of which it is said, 'With you is the fountain of life'? For how shall they thirst, who 'shall be filled with the riches of your house' (Psalm 36:9)?[1]

DIALOGUING WITH THE WORD

At the well of Sychar, the Samaritan woman feels she is understood truly and deeply. Understood, not judged. Understood and loved. Do not be afraid of dialogue with Jesus, your Saviour. To you, too, he promises living water, springing up to eternal life. If you knew the gift of God...

Jesus calls you to bring truth into your life. Allow yourself to be questioned and renewed by his word.

 The Samaritan woman questions Jesus about where and how to worship God and receives an essential response: 'the hour is coming, and is now, when the true worshippers will worship the Father in spirit and truth, for indeed the Father seeks such people to worship Him. God is spirit, and those who worship Him must worship in spirit and truth' (John 4:23–24). No one can block you from this worship of God, present in the temple of your heart.

 In any situation of life, you can worship God in spirit and truth. St Paul exhorts the first Christians to live their existence as worship pleasing to God: 'May your spirit, soul, and body be kept sound and blameless' (1 Thessalonians 5:23), and 'Whether you eat or drink or whether you do not, do everything for the glory of God' (1 Corinthians 10:31).

 The Samaritan woman cannot stop herself from running into town and recounting the extraordinary experience of her encounter with Jesus. What was for her a painful and humiliating situation becomes the starting point for proclamation and witness: 'Come see a man who told me everything I have done! Could this be the Messiah?' (John 4:29). Do you see how important it is to have an experience of Jesus? Have you ever tried to talk about him with a spiritual director or guide?

✛

PAUSE TO PONDER

Let us pray under the guidance of the Spirit, who makes a 'spring of living water' flow within us:

Make us responsive to your thirst, Lord Jesus!
Your 'give me a drink' continues to fill us with astonishment.
The Samaritan woman didn't understand this at first,
marvelling that you, a Jew, should ask her for a drink.
Much less is it understood by those who,
after nailing you to the cross, mocked your thirst.
They wanted to see if Elijah would come to quench your thirst,
and in the end they brought to your mouth a sponge
soaked in vinegar.
Your thirst, Lord, is not slaked with the water of Sychar,
nor your hunger satisfied with the food your disciples bought.
You hunger to fulfil the work of him who sent you,
of him who so loved the world as to give his only-begotten Son.
You thirst and hunger for our salvation.
You, our God, sit at the well
and wait for a sip of water from those who,
without your water, would die of thirst.
Teach us, you, the spring of living water,
to find you where you are,
at the well you have dug deep inside of us.
The Truth lives within us.
Help us, Lord Jesus, to live our lives according to the truth;
teach us to adore the Father in Spirit and truth;
make us your enamoured bride,
who invokes you together with the Spirit:
'The Spirit and the Bride say, "Come."
And let whoever hears say, "Come."
Come, whoever is thirsty,
whoever wants to receive the gift of living water.'
(Revelation 22:17)

✳

Chapter 6

THE GOOD SHEPHERD

The discourse on the good shepherd is among the most fascinating passages of the Gospel (John 10). It is set in Jerusalem, in close proximity to the sign of the healing of the man born blind (John 9). A new scene is not set until 10:19–21, where we again find the theme of 'division' (schísma, also found at 9:16), arising among the listeners, and the themes of blindness and sight.

Jesus came to be the light of the world, the gate of freedom, and the shepherd of life. Some people welcome him and others reject him; some open their eyes and others close them. The entirety of John chapters 9 through 10 is placed within a strong context of 'mission', which is presented as the realisation and manifestation of the works of the Father:

- 9:4: We must do the *works* of the One Who sent me.
- 10:37: If I am not doing my Father's *works*, do not believe me!
- 10:38: If… you do not believe me, believe the *works*.

A LOOK AT THE STRUCTURE

The discourse of the good shepherd opens abruptly, with an 'Amen, amen I say to you' (10:1). In John's language this phrase indicates continuity and development rather than a new beginning. In effect, this discourse continues the account of the man born blind and his dramatic expulsion from the synagogue (9:34). Verses 19 to 21 of chapter 10 deal with the idea of moral blindness, already censured in 9:39–41. Thus the passage is set within the framework of the dramatic overturning of the ideas of seeing/not seeing according to Christ's judgment:

- A: 9:39–41: For judgment I came into this world, so that those who do not see may see, and those who see may become blind.
- B: 10:1–18: Jesus, the gate and the good shepherd.
- A: 9:41: If you were blind you would have no sin, but since you say, 'We see!' your sin remains.

The central passage is divided into two sections, subdivided at verse 6 by the comment from the evangelist: 'Jesus told them this parable [paroimía], but they didn't understand what the things he was telling them meant.' The term paroimía cannot simply be translated as 'parable' or 'allegory'. It means, instead, an obscure and enigmatic discourse, a puzzle that requires explanation. One could call this a revelation divided into two parts, a type of diptych beginning with the same formula:

- Enigmatic statement: Amen, amen, I say to you (vv. 1–5).
- Incomprehension: ... but they did not understand (v. 6).
- Statement of revelation: Amen, amen, I say to you (vv. 7–18).

THE ENIGMATIC DISCOURSE

Let's read the brief enigmatic discourse. It has been very carefully composed and is arranged in a concentric form. It contrasts two figures: on the one hand, the shepherd of the sheep, and on the other hand, the thief and robber, a figure who reappears in verse 5 as the stranger. I will point out several features of the composition of the text: the language of entering/exiting, of walking/following, the emphasis given to listening/voice, and the symbolism of the door:

- A. Amen, amen, I say to you, Whoever doesn't go in by the *gate* into the sheepfold but *enters* by another way, he is a thief and robber.
- B. But whoever comes in by the *gate*, he is the *shepherd* of the sheep. The gatekeeper opens to him, and the sheep *hear his voice*.
- C. He calls his own sheep by name, and *leads them out*. When he drives out all his own sheep he *goes before* them, and the sheep *follow* him because they *know his voice*.
- D. But they do not *follow* a stranger, instead, they flee from him, because they do not *know the voice* of strangers.

The shepherd is contrasted with the thief by the way in which he approaches the sheep: he passes through the gate, which is the normal way to enter the fold. John plays with the symbolic language and its multiple meanings: the word *aule*, which is used to indicate the enclosure for the sheep (that is, the 'sheepfold'), seems also to allude to the 'enclosure' of the temple, the place of the encounter with God. Resuming the discourse, Jesus twice declares openly, 'I am the gate for the sheep!' (vv. 7, 9).

Here we can note many verbs of movement, as well as the vocabulary of the exodus: 'exit' and 'enter' recall the powerful action by which God brought his people out of Egypt to have them enter the promised land. Even the phrase 'he walks ahead', referring to the shepherd, evokes the divine action in the first exodus from Egypt, and in the second from Babylon (see Isaiah 40:11).

A strong affective relationship and mutual understanding exist between the shepherd and the sheep. On the shepherd's part, this relationship calls for personal knowledge ('he calls them by name') and guidance of the sheep ('he leads them out'). The sheep, in turn, listen and follow ('they hear his voice and follow him', vv. 3–4). This type of relationship does not occur with strangers, from whom the sheep 'run away' because 'they do not recognise the voice of strangers'.

These words and images recall the account of Exodus, beginning with the episode on Mount Horeb, where Moses receives the order to bring the people of God out of Egypt (3:10). It also recalls the various reinterpretations that the prophets made of the exodus, especially Ezekiel 34. That text decries the corrupt behaviour of the evil shepherds of Israel, who were responsible for the dispersion of the flock. Ezekiel then contrasts that with a new exodus and a safe pasture in the promised land, thanks to the intervention of the divine Shepherd.

VOICE AND HEARING

In the perspective of the exodus, John presents Jesus above all as the shepherd who listens. Having left the scene after his order to the blind man ('Go wash yourself in the pool of Siloam,' 9:7), Jesus reappears because he has 'heard that they'd thrown him out' (v. 35). 'Give ear, O Shepherd of Israel,' the psalmist pleads (Psalm 80:1), in the firm conviction that the history of liberation begins precisely on the basis of hearing: 'I have heard their cry on account of their taskmasters' (Exodus 3:7). Like the shepherd of the exodus, Jesus hears and goes to seek out the one who has been unjustly marginalised. He 'will not reject' those who come to him, nor will he let anything be lost of what the Father has given him (John 6:37–39). For this reason, he goes to seek the man who has been 'driven away', finds him and leads him to the full confession of messianic faith, revealing himself openly to him, as in the dialogue with the Samaritan woman:

Jesus reveals himself to the healed blind man:
    'You have seen him, and the one who is speaking with you is he.' (9:37)

Jesus reveals himself to the Samaritan woman:
    'I who am speaking to you am he.' (4:26)

I would say that his listening to the Father who so loved the world (3:16) makes Christ capable of an incomparable listening to men and women, in each one's unique nature and situation. And hearing turns into knowledge: 'he calls his own sheep by name' (10:3). This is shown in an eminent way in the encounter of the risen Jesus with Mary Magdalene, who recognises Jesus precisely when he calls her by name: 'Mary!' (20:16; see also 11:28: 'The Teacher is here and he is asking for you').

In biblical language, 'knowing' is not limited to the intellectual sphere but is extended to the emotional life, even including the intimacy that binds husband and wife together. The Lord has known his people with the passion of a man for the woman of his heart (Hosea 2:18–22; Isaiah 54:4–8), with the tenderness of a mother for the fruit of her womb (Isaiah 49:15). A hearing like this calls forth, by its nature, a mutual response: 'and the sheep hear his voice' (John 10:3). Jesus is even able to say accusingly to the Jews, 'You do not believe because you are not from among my sheep. My sheep listen to my voice, and I know them' (10:26–27).

A kind of natural relationship is manifested between being a sheep and hearing, as if the urgent appeal 'Hear, O Israel!' found its fulfilment in becoming a believer. In John 10, Jesus does not order us to hear him. He does not say, 'My sheep, listen!' but rather, 'They will listen to my voice', meaning that they believe and trust in him. It is not a matter of bravado but of grace; it is a gift of the Father who draws one to Christ. 'I am the *good* shepherd,' Jesus says, 'and I know mine and mine know me, just as the Father knows me and I know the Father' (vv. 14–15). There is such mutual intimacy between him and his sheep that it resembles the loving knowledge that eternally binds the Father to the Son and the Son to the Father.

HE LEADS THEM OUT AND WALKS AHEAD OF THEM

The scene of the shepherd who, in the morning, leads his flock out from the sheepfold (10:3b–4) was a familiar one in the Palestine of Jesus' time. That image hearkens back to another 'exit' that radically marked Israel's history: the exit from slavery. In the development of this *paroimía*, Jesus appears as the shepherd who is able to lead the entire adventure of the exodus, playing the part of both Moses (the 'leading out') and Joshua (the 'entering' into the promised land). In fact, after presenting himself as the gate, he affirms, 'Whoever comes in through me will be saved, and will enter and leave and find pasture' (10:9).

Christ is the gate[1] who gives access to the Father, and in this sense he is the way to life (14:6). Those who enter through him find salvation and 'pasture' because they approach the very fountain of life (see Revelation 7:17). In a singular interweaving of symbols, Jesus presents himself here as the gate, which then becomes the shepherd: not only an entryway, but a guide and leader, 'the pioneer (*archegós*) of their salvation' (Hebrews 2:10).[2] Through him and with his guidance, one can genuinely exit from the prison of egoism (personal and collective) and from the various forms of slavery, to enter into the land of freedom.

As Yahweh brought his people out of Egypt while walking ahead of them (Deuteronomy 1:30; Psalm 68:8), so also the good shepherd, Jesus, brings his sheep out and walks before them. His behaviour calls forth a new reciprocity. The sheep, in fact, are not exhorted to follow the shepherd, just as they are not exhorted to hear him. The situation is simply factual: the one who is my sheep hears; the one who is my sheep follows. For John, it is inconceivable to imagine a believer who does not follow: the shepherd walks ahead and the sheep come behind him; they follow him.

This perspective clearly and strongly recalls the exodus from Egypt, and at the same time it orients the view toward the definitive exodus that Jesus accomplishes in his death and resurrection.

In fact, 'his hour' is drawing near: he is about to pass from 'this world for the Father' (John 13:1). But the hour of his disciples is also drawing near, symbolically illustrated by the 'hour' of the woman who is about to give birth. Her suffering is destined to be transformed into joy as soon as the child comes to light (16:21).

THAT THEY MIGHT HAVE LIFE

The figure most closely associated to that of a shepherd is the figure of a mother. One could speak of the maternal aspect of God, of his tender care for life: 'I have come that you might have life and have it abundantly' (John 10:10). Who better than a mother can exemplify the vocation of giving life, making room within one's own being, generating and nourishing? A shepherd's vigilance recalls a mother's watchfulness over the fruit of her womb, her creature.

How many came before Jesus, claiming messianic authority, only to be revealed as 'thieves and robbers'?[3] They raised false hopes, they promised life and freedom, but in fact they led the people along the way of death. The messianism of one like Barabbas is theft and robbery. Jesus never resorts to weapons.[4] On the contrary, in order that the sheep might have life, he lays down his own (10:11, 15). This is the height of solidarity: a life 'given for others'.[5]

This 'being for' means complete availability, an utter self-giving to the point of laying down one's own life for others. The life offered by the good shepherd therefore comes at a high price, but it is overabundant: he came 'that you might have life and have it abundantly' (John 10:10). It is like the wine offered abundantly in Cana (six jars filled to the brim, John 2:7), like the Spirit that Christ gives 'without measure' (3:34), like the bread and fish distributed to the 5000, who ate until they were satisfied (6:11–12). Jesus gives his life freely:

'This is why the Father loves me,
because I lay down my life
in order to take it up again.
No one takes it from me;
On the contrary, I lay it down on my own.
I have power to lay it down
and I have power to take it up again.
This is the command I have received from my Father.'
(10:17–18)

One who is able to give and take back is not a slave. He acts as a slave, but he is a lord, as is stated explicitly when Jesus, in order to wash the disciples' feet, 'laid aside his cloak' and then 'put his cloak back on' and declared, 'You call me "The Teacher" and "The Lord", and rightly so, because I am' (13:13). The sovereign freedom of Jesus in giving his life for his sheep constitutes the 'command' that he received from the Father, and also the reason why the Father loves him. By doing this, he brings the sheep into the relationship of mutual knowledge that he himself has with the Father.

'I HAVE OTHER SHEEP'

The vision of Christ expands, extending to the great plan of the Father, who wishes to gather the entire human family together. In the perspective of the servant of whom Isaiah speaks, he feels that his mission cannot be limited to Israel:

'I have other sheep who are not of this fold,
and I must lead them,
and they will listen to my voice, and become
one flock, one shepherd.' (10:16)

The Father who so loved the world as to give his only begotten Son (3:16) wants him to lay down his life 'so that the scattered children of God might gather into one' (11:52). In John 10, this is clearly seen in its twofold designation: 'my sheep', meaning Israel, and 'other sheep who are not of this fold', meaning the non-Jews, both Samaritans and pagans.[6] All of them have been given by the Father to Jesus (10:29; 17:2, 7, 9, 24), the true Servant of the Lord:

[H]e says, 'It is too light a thing
that you should be my servant
to raise up the tribes of Jacob
and to restore the survivors of Israel;
I will give you as a light to the nations,
that my salvation may reach
to the ends of the earth.' (Isaiah 49:6)

It is not said of the 'other sheep' that they will be united with the flock of Israel, but simply that they will be 'led'. This verb summarises the task of the good shepherd as previously described in contrast with the strangers, thieves, robbers and hired men (John 10:1–13). The response of the 'other sheep' is indicated by the phrase 'listen to my voice', exactly as is said of the sheep that Jesus calls 'my sheep' (10:27). Therefore the care and dedication he has demonstrated toward Israel exemplify his universal mission, the sign and instrument of the Father's salvation plan.

Jesus does not unite the flock by leading them all into the same sheepfold. This is presented, instead, as a future goal: 'become one flock, one shepherd' (10:16). The unity towards which the various flocks are moving does not, therefore, remove their individual characteristics and differences. It is based, instead, on the principle of unity that is a person: 'one shepherd'. They will become one flock if they follow the one good shepherd, although they follow different paths and gather in different sheepfolds. This is the unity for which Christ prays on the evening of his death: 'So that all may be one, just as You, Father, are in me and I in You, so they, too, may be in Us, so the world may believe that You sent me' (17:21).

DIALOGUING WITH THE WORD

Let's imagine ourselves at the 'Sheep Gate' in Jerusalem, near the pool that was called the *Probatica* (or 'of the sheep'), just a few steps from the temple enclosure. Let's imagine Jesus approaching the blind man whose sight he had restored, who had been 'cast out' of the community of Jewish faith because of his courageous witness to the events of his healing. Cast out by the shepherds of God's flock, he finds himself at the same time 'seeing' and 'a stray sheep'.

Jesus poses the fundamental question to the formerly blind man: 'Do you believe in the Son of Man?' This question is also posed to me—and not by just anyone, but by Jesus himself. 'Son of Man' is the title that identifies him according to the vision of the prophets, in particular Daniel 7:13–14. What is my answer to his question? The man Jesus addresses is caught off guard, but he does not offer a standard answer. Instead, he frankly asks for help; he wants to know who this Son of Man is. I should not be afraid to pose questions to Jesus in prayer: 'Who are you, my God, that you consider yourself the Son of Man?'

Jesus is the 'gate for the sheep', meaning all of his disciples. Passing through him means passing from death to life, from slavery to freedom, from darkness to light, from the sadness of egoism to the joy of love. He is, in fact, the gate that gives access to heaven, to the bosom of the Father. Through baptism, I have passed through Christ, the gate of salvation. It is also necessary to pass through him in order to exercise true pastoral action, to be not thieves and robbers but servants of the good of others. Christ, who is the door of salvation and freedom, makes me go out and come in: I go out from myself in order to enter within God, go out from myself in order to enter into contact with my brothers and sisters.

How do I live my relationship with Jesus, who calls me by my name? He knows me like no other, with the same profundity with which he is known by and knows the Father. He wants to involve me in this loving knowledge, so that I can feel myself completely known and loved by him. He came for me; he is my good shepherd. How much do I trust in him? To whom do I go in order to have life in abundance?

Jesus does not keep his passion hidden. He has a great dream: he desires to gather into one all the dispersed children of God, in a single flock with a single shepherd. He is ready to give his life to fulfil this dream. He lays down his own life so that all may have full, superabundant life. Do I feel myself a participant in this great passion of the good shepherd? How do I live out the call to follow Jesus in taking care of others, in particular the smallest and the least?

✜

PAUSE TO PONDER

Thank the good shepherd for the abundant table that he prepares for you every day. Pray Psalm 23 slowly.

The Lord is my shepherd,
I shall not want.
He makes me lie down in green pastures;
he leads me beside still waters;
he restores my soul.
He leads me in right paths
for his name's sake.

Even though I walk through the darkest valley,
I fear no evil; for you are with me;
your rod and your staff—they comfort me.

You prepare a table before me
in the presence of my enemies;
you anoint my head with oil; my cup overflows.
Surely goodness and mercy shall follow me
all the days of my life,
and I shall dwell in the house of the Lord
my whole life long.

Make your own this prayer of Father James Alberione:

I thank you, O Jesus, Good Shepherd,
who came down from heaven to seek out the human race
and bring it back to the way of salvation.
In you the promise is fulfilled:
'I will raise up in the midst of the scattered sheep
a shepherd who will gather them together and feed them.'
The shepherd walks before the flock
and the sheep follow him because they know his voice.
Have mercy on those who nourish themselves
on lies and vanity.
Call sinners back to your way.
Support the wavering, strengthen the weak.
May all follow you,
O shepherd and guardian of our souls.
You alone are life,
you alone have words of eternal life.
I will follow you anywhere.[7]

*

Chapter 7

LAZARUS, MARTHA, AND MARY: FRIENDSHIP AND RESURRECTION

Bethany, house of friendship, is where Jesus must have found himself in good company among Martha, Lazarus, and Mary. When in Jerusalem, Jesus usually stayed with them. Even six days before his passion he was with them (John 12:1–8). John insists on the affective dimension that runs between the Master and this unique community of a brother and two sisters. Nothing is said of their parents, nor of any marriage relations. The three seem to form a perfect unity in diversity.

Martha, which in Aramaic means 'owner', shows herself to be an excellent hostess. According to Luke, she is the older sister and also the owner of the house.[1] Her character is the opposite of Mary's: Martha is the busy hostess, while Mary is the one sitting and listening. Martha is a woman open to the newness of Jesus. She allows his word to question her and arrives at a confession of faith that is among the loftiest in the Gospel and parallels Peter's.

Lazarus is explicitly presented as a 'friend' of Jesus. Yet Jesus does not run to his friend's bedside when the sisters tell him that Lazarus is seriously ill. Why does Jesus not respond in kind to Martha and Mary? What does it mean to Jesus to care about someone?

Mary is a preeminent symbol of the woman who loves. The evangelist John introduces her as an icon of *agape*, with a reference to later events: 'Mary was the one who had anointed the Lord with oil and wiped his feet dry with her hair' (John 11:2). This episode actually takes place in the following chapter, during the supper in honour of Lazarus, who had been raised from the dead. So, in theory, the reader does not yet know about it. Why, then, this preview? What appears here is a bit of the shared wisdom of the evangelist's community, where Mary is identified by her gesture of love: she is the one who intuited beforehand, with the foreknowledge of the heart, the nearness of Jesus' death.

THE QUESTION OF LIFE AND DEATH

John 11 faces the central question of life and death. Jesus claims to be the passageway from death to life: he not only resurrects but he is the 'resurrection' (*anástasis*); he is the 'life' (*zoe*, definitively removed from the power of death).

Only John speaks of the illness and subsequent death and resurrection of Lazarus. The synoptic Gospels report two other miracles: the resurrection of Jairus' daughter (Mark 6:35–43) and the resurrection of the only son of the widow of Nain (Luke 7:11–17). Nonetheless, Lazarus' resurrection (as well as those recounted by the synoptic Gospels) is the return to a life that will again see death. Therefore, it differs greatly from the resurrection of Jesus, which knows no precedent in the history of salvation.

Let us enter into the flow of the narrative to understand the message the evangelist intends to offer us through the sign of the death and resurrection of Lazarus. We can divide the passage into four scenes: the first (vv. 1–16) tells about the illness of Lazarus and Jesus' strange response to the news; the second (vv. 17–27) is the dialogue between Jesus and Martha; the third (vv. 28–37) highlights the weeping of Mary and Jesus; the fourth (vv. 38–43) takes place at the tomb of Lazarus, whom Jesus calls back to life.

'LORD, YOUR FRIEND IS SICK'

The account opens with a bit of news that would be too ordinary if it were not for the emotional bonds that are in play: 'Now a certain man was sick, Lazarus of Bethany, from the village of Mary and her sister Martha' (11:1). The relationships of friendship and the singular affection of Mary take centre stage (v. 2).

A message goes out from the house of friendship so dear to the Master. The two sisters send word: 'Lord, behold, the one you love is sick' (v. 3). How does Jesus react to this news? In a surprising way, as found elsewhere in the Gospel. He responds, 'This sickness will not bring death—it is for the glory of God so the Son of Man may be glorified through it' (v. 4). It is likely that the messengers do not understand these words; nor do Jesus' disciples. For his part, the evangelist takes pains to restate, 'Now Jesus loved Martha and her sister and Lazarus' (v. 5). In effect, his way of loving is decisively original. He does not run to Lazarus's bedside but stays another two days in the place where he received the news. Only on the third day—a detail that should be noted—does he finally say to his disciples, 'Let us go into Judea again.' They react strongly: 'Rabbi, the Jews were just now trying to stone you, and you are going back there again?' (vv. 7–8).

With great serenity and awareness, Jesus responds that one must walk while it is day. He then reveals Lazarus's situation: 'Our friend Lazarus has fallen asleep, but I am going now to wake him up' (v. 11). The disciples interpret this expression literally, commenting, 'Lord, if he has fallen asleep he will recover' (v. 12). They are speaking on different levels, as the evangelist notes: 'But Jesus had spoken about his death, while they thought he was speaking about natural sleep' (v. 13).

This misinterpretation is followed by the Master's clear statement: 'Lazarus has died, and I rejoice for your sake that I was not there, so you may believe. But let us go to him' (vv. 14–15). This scene concludes with Thomas, who understands the risk, encouraging his companions: 'Let us go, too, to die with him!' (v. 16).

'LORD, IF YOU HAD BEEN HERE'

The second scene presents Jesus' arrival in Bethany. The evangelist tells us the distance from Bethany to Jerusalem ('about two miles') and that 'many of the Jews had come to Martha and Mary to console them over their brother' (vv. 18–19). One can read between the lines that Lazarus must have been known and respected in the capital. Martha is the first to be informed that Jesus has arrived: 'So Martha, when she heard that Jesus was coming, met him, but Mary stayed in the house' (v. 20).

The meeting with the Master is set outdoors, outside the village. Martha speaks first, with a veiled reproach:

'Lord, if you had been here my brother would not have died! But even now I know that whatever you ask God for, God will give you.'

Jesus said to her, 'Your brother will rise!' (vv. 21–23)

This intense, fast-paced dialogue unfolds over a total of five passages (Martha intervenes three times, Jesus two). It culminates in a solemn profession of faith that parallels Peter's in John 6:68–69.

We should first note the point of departure. Like many Jews of her time, Martha believed in the resurrection of the dead. She does not doubt that her brother will rise in eschatological time: 'I know that he will rise at the resurrection on the last day' (v. 24).

Here Martha expresses a faith that is part of her environment. The development of faith in the resurrection had undoubtedly been fostered by the book of Daniel, in which we read, 'Many of those who sleep in the dust of the earth shall awake, some to everlasting life, and some to shame and everlasting contempt' (Daniel 12:2).[2]

Faith in the resurrection is also attested to in the second book of Maccabees (one of the deuterocanonical books of the Bible, accepted as part of scripture by the Catholic and Orthodox Churches). We recall in particular the atrocious martyrdom of a mother and her seven sons. In the midst of his tortures, one of them says to his executioner, 'You accursed wretch, you dismiss us from this present life, but the King of the universe will raise us up to an everlasting renewal of life' (2 Maccabees 7:9). And another adds, 'One cannot but choose to die at the hands of mortals and to cherish the hope God gives of being raised again by him. But for you there will be no resurrection to life!' (v. 14). So the martyrs will receive new and eternal life, but this will be denied to the unjust and the persecutors. For them, death will be eternal, meaning definitive.

At Jesus' time, many of the Pharisees believed in the resurrection but, paradoxically, the priests contested this belief, though not all of them. The Sadducees, who were rich and belonged to the hierarchy in power at the time, did.[3] Some of them question Jesus maliciously, presenting to him the case of the widow who, in accordance with the law of the Levirate, marries seven brothers in succession: 'When they rise at the resurrection whose wife will she be?—all seven brothers had her as wife' (Mark 12:23).

Jesus unmasks the Sadducees' presumption and reinvigorates faith in the resurrection on the basis of the scriptures, which attest to a vital relationship with God:

Jesus said to them, 'Isn't this the reason you go astray, that you understand neither the Scriptures nor the power of God? For when you rise from the dead you neither marry nor are given in marriage, but are like the angels in Heaven. But as for the dead rising, have you not read in the scroll of Moses, at the passage about the thorn bush, how God spoke to him, and said, *I am the God of Abraham and the God of Isaac and the God of Jacob?* He is not God of the dead but of the living; you have gone seriously astray.' (Mark 12:24–27)[4]

Returning to our account, Jesus replies to Martha, 'I am the resurrection and the life! Whoever believes in me, even if he should die, will live, and everyone who lives and believes in me shall never die!' (John 11:25–26).

Jesus himself is the one who will raise on the last day those who have believed in him (see John 5:24–25; 6:40), and already he gives a sign of this by bringing Lazarus back to life. But Jesus does not come to prolong physical life by suppressing death or delaying it indefinitely. He does not compete with physicians or with science. The reason he came was to communicate the life that he himself possesses: divine, indestructible life. For this reason, he begins his reply with the divine Name: 'I Am'. Jesus is the resurrection because he is the life. Martha hoped in a faraway resurrection, at the end of time, but Jesus identifies himself with the resurrection that is already taking place, in the dynamism of the new life (Spirit) that he communicates to us. Jesus addresses Martha directly and personally: 'Do you believe this?' She immediately replies, 'Yes, Lord, I have come to believe that you are the Messiah, the Son of God who has come into the world!' (v. 27).

Martha allows Jesus to lead her on this uphill journey. She passes from faith in the resurrection of the dead as the Jewish world believed in it to the recognition that Jesus himself is the resurrection: to live in him is to pass from death to life.

'THE MASTER IS HERE AND IS ASKING FOR YOU'

When Mary enters the scene, the situation becomes even more emotionally charged. The few words that Martha speaks quietly to Mary go straight to the heart: 'The Teacher is here and he is asking for you' (v. 28). Mary gets up in haste and runs to him. She reaches the Teacher, throws herself at his feet and pours out her anguish in the same words Martha had used: 'Lord, if you had been here my brother would not have died!' (v. 32). She is of the same mind as Martha and, indirectly, expresses to the Master her disappointment with his incomprehensible absence. Jesus does not reply. Seeing her weep, he too is deeply moved. He 'groaned in spirit and was troubled' (v. 33).

It is a distinctly human scene. There are no arguments. Jesus does not say a word. Mary's weeping troubles and touches him: 'So when Jesus saw her weeping, and the Jews who had come with her weeping, he groaned in spirit and was troubled.' The evangelist uses the verb *tarásso*, which conveys the profound distress experienced in the face of death. This echoes a passage from the Old Testament, from the book of Lamentations: '[God] has blocked my ways with hewn stones, he has made my paths crooked [troubled/distressed]' (3:9).

The path walled up with stone seems to allude to the tomb. The mind and the heart shudder in the face of that blocked path, which precludes the return to life. We should not forget that at the beginning of the account, John anticipated Mary's anointing of Jesus with oil: the figure of Mary cannot be separated from her gesture of love and Jesus' interpretation of it, relating it to his own 'burial' (John 12:7). In the presence of Mary, who is weeping over the death of Lazarus, Jesus also experiences distress and anguish over his own death and burial. We find that same verb, *tarásso*, on the lips of Jesus in the following chapter, when he exclaims, 'Now my soul is troubled! And what shall I say? "Father, save me from this hour"? But it was for *this* that I came to this hour' (John 12:27).

But Jesus does not give in to distress. Although he certainly experiences it in all of its bitterness, so to speak, he nevertheless reacts; he questions. He wants to go to the site of death's victory and to confront it directly. '"Where have you laid him?" They said to him, "Lord, come and see!"' (v. 34).

'UNTIE HIM AND LET HIM GO'

Jesus goes to the tomb, 'again groaning' (v. 38). The Master is not ashamed to weep and to display his sorrow openly over his friend's death. He, too, mourns. One should not interpret this as an empty show of emotion because Jesus knew that Lazarus would rise. On the contrary, if the evangelist dwells upon these aspects, it is evidently because he intends to show Jesus in all his humanity.

The tomb was a cave, against which a stone had been placed, according to the custom of the time. Jesus gives an order: 'Take the stone away!' Martha shudders, 'Lord, by now he will smell—it has been four days!' (v. 39). The entire scene is very human. Martha reacts instinctively, seeming to have completely forgotten the faith she had proclaimed earlier.[5] But Jesus replies: 'Did not I tell you that if you believe you will see the glory of God?' (v. 40).

'So they took the stone away' (v. 41). This is the moment of intense and trusting prayer. Jesus does not ask for anything at all; he is certain the Father hears him: 'Father, I give You thanks, because You heard me. Now I knew that You always hear me, but I said this for the sake of the crowd standing around me, so they may believe that You sent me' (vv. 41–42). The resurrection of Lazarus is thus recounted as a sign for our faith. At this point, we understand better the meaning of Jesus' words: 'This sickness will not bring death—it is for the glory of God so the Son of Man may be glorified through it.' The prayer of Jesus is directed toward the fulfilment of the work the Father has entrusted to him: 'For just as the Father raises the dead and gives them life, so too the Son gives life to those he wants to' (John 5:21).

After praying, Jesus cries out in a loud voice: 'Lazarus, come out!' The dead man emerges, with his feet and hands bound in burial bands and his face wrapped in cloth. Jesus tells them, 'Untie him and let him go' (v. 44).

Lazarus responds immediately to Jesus' authoritative words. But the second command is addressed to those present, to the Christian community, to each one of us: 'Untie him.' This means 'free him from the trappings of death'. Lazarus emerges from the tomb like a mummy, his hands and feet tied with the burial bands. Jesus has snatched him from the jaws of death, but it is up to his sisters and those present to do the rest.

THE BANQUET, THE PERFUME, AND LOVE

What happens after the resurrection of Lazarus? How does Jesus behave? How does his friend who has come back to life react? What of his sisters? The evangelist loves bringing us back to the places where Jesus has performed his miracles. This has been seen in connection with Cana, where a second sign is intentionally set following the first, and this will also be the case with Bethany, where John brings us back six days before the Passover (John 12:1–11).

The plot to kill the Master is already underway in Jerusalem. According to the Gospel of Matthew, he himself informs his disciples about the seriousness of the moment: 'You know that the Passover will be in two days, and the Son of Man will be handed over to be crucified' (Matthew 26:2). His enemies are waiting for the right moment, and he withdraws to stay with his friends in Bethany. John agrees with the Synoptics in indicating Bethany as the location of the banquet and of his anointing in relation to his burial. But while Mark and Matthew set the banquet in the home of a certain 'Simon the leper', John takes us to Martha's house. The banquet also serves to celebrate the return from the dead of Jesus' friend Lazarus, who is seated among the dinner company. Martha serves at table, while Mary surprises everyone with a gesture of enormous symbolic importance: she pours a pound of perfumed oil, valuable aromatic nard, over the feet of Jesus (John 12:3). Disregarding what those present might say, she dedicates all of her attention to those feet, caressing them, kissing them and drying them with her long hair.[6]

Judas loudly protests against the wastefulness of this gesture. From his point of view, he is right. That perfume could indeed have been sold for 'three hundred denarii': ten times the price he accepted to 'hand over' the Master! The contrast could not be any more strident. If Mary is an eminent example of *agape*, Judas is the opposite.

But Jesus defends Mary (vv. 7–8). After silently receiving the eloquent gesture of love, he now speaks in her defence. Hadn't Jesus dedicated his entire life to the poor? But who is poorer than he, about to be sold by Judas, abandoned by his own disciples and handed over to death? Mary has understood what is happening. This woman resembles Jesus in that her love knows no limits and she spares no expense. She could have used just enough perfume to honour the guest and bring a touch of celebration to the house. But Mary has poured out all of her perfume, not caring about the criticism from those around her. Jesus appreciates this extravagance, and it is clear why: here the 'wastefulness' shows her measure of love. The logic of love is to give everything, without measure.

DIALOGUING WITH THE WORD

Let's imagine ourselves in Bethany, in the company of Lazarus, Martha, and Mary. Friendship with Jesus brings the flavour of eternity to life. Jesus does not spare his friends from suffering and death. Reason would be happy to overcome death without having to face it, to live without experiencing it. But the mysterious plan of the Father chooses instead, for Jesus and for us, another way of salvation: sickness, suffering, and death are overcome and conquered only after they have been faced.

 How do I live in situations of weakness and sickness? Do I turn to the Father with Jesus' unconditional trust?

 In situations of suffering and death, Jesus asks us the question he posed to Martha: do you believe this? Do you believe that I am the Resurrection and the Life? Resurrection does not mean reincarnation, nor does it simply mean the survival of the soul.

After his resurrection, Lazarus will see death again, while the words of Jesus promise eternal life. The preface for the Catholic funeral service says, 'Life is not taken away, but transformed.' Life is not transformed only after death, but now, during earthly existence. St Paul wonderfully expresses this concept: 'Although our outer self is wasting away, our inner self is being renewed, day by day' (2 Corinthians 4:16). The inevitable disintegration of the body corresponds to the fullness of maturity, and the death of the cells to indestructible life. Am I aware of this splendid transformation to which I am called? How do I live the hope of eternal life?

Only love lasts for ever, because God is love. I must live a risen life now, one illuminated from within by love. What signs of death and resurrection are present in my life?

Mary's perfumed oil is not lost in the air, but in a certain sense it impregnates the walls of the house of Bethany. That perfume is a prelude to the resurrection; it is a love that gives itself completely. Is this perfume present in my family and community?

✛

PAUSE TO PONDER

At the feet of Jesus, like Mary of Bethany, let us allow our hearts to pour forth generously the perfume of love. The Master knows what is inside us. He knows our suffering and our hope. He who called Lazarus out of the tomb did not draw back from being buried himself in the heart of the earth. He knows death by having crossed through it personally. Let us thank him in the words of the psalmist:

Protect me, O God, for in you I take refuge.
I say to the Lord, 'You are my Lord;
I have no good apart from you.'

As for the holy ones in the land, they are the noble,
in whom is all my delight.

Those who choose another god multiply their sorrows;
their drink offerings of blood I will not pour out
or take their names upon my lips.

The Lord is my chosen portion and my cup;
you hold my lot.
The boundary lines have fallen for me in pleasant places;
I have a goodly heritage.
I bless the Lord who gives me counsel;
in the night also my heart instructs me.
I keep the Lord always before me;
because he is at my right hand, I shall not be moved.

Therefore my heart is glad, and my soul rejoices;
my body also rests secure.
For you do not give me up to Sheol,
or let your faithful one see the Pit.

You show me the path of life.
In your presence there is fullness of joy;
in your right hand are pleasures forevermore. (Psalm 16)

＊

Chapter 8

THE LORD BECOMES
A SERVANT

After the banquet in Bethany and the anointing by Mary with the overabundant perfume, the supreme hour of Jesus rapidly approaches. It is the hour of his passion, of the humiliation of his royalty, which is nonetheless exalted because it is from the height of the cross that the Son of Man draws all to himself.

KNOWING THAT HIS HOUR HAD COME

'Before the festival of the Passover, Jesus, knowing that his hour had come to leave this world for the Father, having loved his own in the world, loved them to the end' (John 13:1).

The 'hour' of Jesus is given maximum emphasis, and it frames the entire section that is set in the upper room: 13:1—17:26. Although points of tension are not lacking, these five chapters form a literary unit: they present a unity of place (the upper room), of audience (the Twelve), of time (Jesus' last night with his disciples), of circumstance (the common meal), and of purpose (a farewell gathering). The material is highly varied. It combines narrative passages and bits of dialogue, like the washing of the feet and the denunciation of the traitor (ch. 13), with discursive passages. These contain brief questions from the apostles and lengthy replies from Jesus (chs. 14—16). Finally there is Jesus' long solitary prayer (ch. 17).

At the end of chapter 14, Jesus tells his disciples, 'Get up, let us be going' (v. 31). According to this expression, Jesus is calling for his companions to get up from the table and leave the upper room. But in fact, chapters 15—17 are still set in the upper room. The change of scene actually takes place in 18:1: 'After Jesus said these things he went out with his disciples.'

Without delving into historical-critical research, we are content to affirm here the literary unity of these five chapters set in the room of the Last Supper. Our attention is focused on Jesus, who is fully aware that he is facing the decisive hour for which the Father sent him into the world. And Jesus lives this hour, meaning his passion and death, in the fullness of love. Without evasion of any kind, he continues moving forward on the journey of love until the very end, in an unmistakable style:

During the banquet, when the Devil had already put it into the heart of Judas son of Simon Iscariot to hand Jesus over, knowing that the Father had given all things into his hands and that he had come from God and was now returning to God, he got up from the banquet and laid aside his cloak, and he took a towel and wrapped it around himself. Then he poured water into the washbasin and began to wash the disciples' feet and wipe them dry with the towel he had wrapped around himself. (John 13:2–5)

Not a word. Silence and inexpressible amazement surround the sovereign gesture of the Master who *rises, takes off* his garment, *girds* himself, *pours* the water into the basin, and begins *washing* and *drying* his disciples' feet. Six actions. It is a sequence that seems to echo the six days of the new creation. Nothing like this had ever been seen before. Amazement, emotion, confusion, embarrassment. When Peter's turn comes, he explodes with the first words spoken after a long sequence of solitary actions:

When he came to Simon Peter, Peter said to him, 'Lord, are *you* going to wash *my* feet?' Jesus answered and said to him, 'What I am doing you do not understand just now, but later you will understand.' Peter said to him, 'You will *never* wash my feet!' Jesus answered him, 'Unless I wash you, you will have no share in me.' Simon Peter said to him, 'Lord, wash not only my feet, but my hands and head as well!' (13:6–9)

Peter wants to draw back; he does not accept that Jesus would lower himself like a slave. He calls him 'Lord', a title that clearly contrasts with the washing of feet, the task of a slave. Humility is one thing, but this gesture is excessive.[1]

The Master's response explains that this is not simply a matter of 'humility'. What is at stake is having a part in him, sharing his plan for the kingdom, which is decisively different from the world's parameters. For Jesus, the greatest one is the one who serves.

Peter replies in turn. Separating himself from Jesus is out of the question! In order to stay with him, he is willing to do whatever Jesus wants: 'Lord, wash not only my feet, but my hands and head as well!' The impetuous Peter is willing to be washed all over— but does he understand his Master? Jesus responds by saying, 'Whoever has bathed has no need to wash except for his feet.' This seems to correct the perspective of the disciple who still thinks in Jewish terms. Jesus' gesture does not have the significance of a rite of purification, but indicates the style of service that is integral to his community. For this reason, he expressly calls the attention of his disciples to this emblematic gesture:

'Do you understand what I have done for you? You call me "The Teacher" and "The Lord", and rightly so, because I am. So if I, the Lord and Teacher, have washed your feet, you, too, ought to wash each others' feet, because I have given you an example so that, just as I have done for you, you, too, should do.' (vv. 12–15)

Loving means putting oneself at the service of others, as Jesus did, in a spirit of complete welcome and availability: 'As I have loved you, you too should love one another' (v. 34). This is the identification card of the disciples of Jesus, the unmistakable sign of belonging to his school: 'All will know by this that you are my disciples, if you have love for one another' (v. 35).

Bishop Tonino Bello loved to talk about the 'Church of the apron': 'The Church of the apron does not absolutise high levels of agreement. In the "hit parade" of preferences, the most successful image of the Church seems to be the one that represents it with the lectionary in its hands, or with the chasuble on.'[2] And yet the apron is one of the vestments that Jesus used at that solemn eucharistic meal on Holy Thursday. The stole and the apron are like the two sides of a single sacramental coin. Without the apron, the stole would only be a decoration. Without the stole, the apron would be barren. And so Bello encouraged a return to the path of service, which is the path of compassionate kindness, of *synkatábasi*, of sharing.

JESUS, THE WAY, THE TRUTH, AND THE LIFE

Jesus does not think of himself as the hour of his passion is drawing near. He thinks, instead, of encouraging and supporting the community of the disciples whom he calls 'friends'. He thinks of each of us. Anxiety and fear must not have the upper hand in this dramatic situation, but instead complete self-entrustment to the Father and lively faith in Jesus: 'Let not your hearts be troubled! Believe in God and believe in me' (John 14:1).

Jesus is about to be taken from his friends but he does not at all intend to abandon them. He is about to accomplish his Passover, or the passage 'to leave this world for the Father' (13:1), and the purpose of his 'going' to the Father is that of preparing a place for them as well:

'In my Father's house are many rooms; were it not so, would I have told you that I am going to prepare a place for you? And if I go and prepare a place for you, I will come again and take you to myself, so that where I am, you too may be. Yet where I am going, you know the way.' (14:2–4)

To go beyond the immediately apparent meaning, to delve into the deep meaning of things: this is the art of Jesus with his disciples right up to the very end. The last sentence of the passage above is intentionally provocative. In fact, Thomas objects: 'Lord, we do not know where you are going! How can we know the way?' (v. 5).

The answer is very direct, with the vigour of a formula that has no equal in the scriptures: 'I am the way (hodós) and the truth (aletheia) and the life (zoe).' And he adds, 'No one comes to the Father except through me' (v. 6). This statement is composed in the form of a chiasm: the first person pronoun (I/me) at the beginning and end, and at the centre the theme of the way and of going to the Father:

a   I am
     b   the way and the truth and the life.
     c   No one comes to the Father
a'   except through me.

As is typical of the fourth Gospel, this discourse moves along two levels. Thomas uses the term hodós, 'way', in the material sense, as a path to be travelled physically. But Jesus speaks of hodós in the spiritual sense, as the possibility of access to the Father and of personal participation in the mystery of God.[3] In other words, he presents himself as the sole mediator between God and men.[4] The ability to travel between heaven and earth is assured by the humanity of Jesus. One ascends to the Father only by means of the incarnate Word.

But Jesus also declares that he is the truth: not 'a' truth, but 'the' truth, the authentic truth in its fullness. This is a particularly important declaration, one that was anticipated in the Prologue: 'For the Torah was given through Moses, grace and truth came through Jesus Christ' (1:17). The incarnate Word is 'full of grace and truth'. The word 'grace', *cháris* in Greek, leads back to the Hebrew word *chésed*, which means 'benevolence, mercy'. 'Truth', *aletheia* in Greek, corresponds to the Hebrew word *emèt*, which means 'fidelity'.[5]

John and the other believers contemplate in Jesus the complete and definitive revelation of the mercy and fidelity of God. They contemplate the splendid manifestation of his face, of his profound truth: because God is Love. Father James Alberione used to teach:

To model ourselves always upon the definition that Jesus gave of himself: 'I am the way, the truth, and the life.' What does this mean? It means that all spiritual work, and also study, and then the apostolate in a preeminent way, must incorporate the spirit that is indicated in this definition: Jesus the Master, way, truth, and life.[6]

'IT WAS NOT YOU WHO CHOSE ME'

St Thomas Aquinas observes, 'It is normal among human beings that each one attributes to himself the cause of friendship, according to the words of Sirach (37:1): "Every friend declares: I am the one who has established friendship."'[7] But can we advance the same claim in regard to Jesus? 'You did not choose me; on the contrary, I chose you' (15:16), the Master recalls to his disciples in the intimate setting of the upper room.

It is Jesus who claims primacy in this choice. *Not you... but I*: the antithesis is clear. It is as if Jesus wants to eliminate any naive and narcissistic pretence. He takes the initiative in this choice, unlike in Jewish society at the time, where disciples chose their own rabbi, their teacher.[8] But in the New Testament, it is Jesus who calls, who decides the where and the how of his own following.[9]

The first meaning of the word *eklégomai*, 'elect', signifies a calling from/among (*ek*) and therefore implies separation from others, preference, being chosen. In the background we can glimpse the biblical theme of divine election. The choice of God always comes first, just as the call precedes the response. God calls Abraham in order to bless all nations in him (Genesis 18:19). With sovereign freedom, he chooses Israel from among all peoples of the earth. This is not because they are better than others, but instead it is a question of love: 'It was not because you were more numerous than any other people that the Lord set his heart on you and chose you—for you were the fewest of all peoples. It was because the Lord loved you' (Deuteronomy 7:7–8).

Chosen from among the nations as 'a people holy to the Lord', his exclusive property (Deuteronomy 14:2), Israel is called in its turn to correspond to this love, to choose Yahweh. This is what happens at the foot of Mount Sinai and in the great assembly of Shechem, where the people declare, 'The Lord our God we will serve, and him we will obey' (Joshua 24:24).

God chooses first, but he wants reciprocity; he wants covenant. He reveals his own name to Moses (Exodus 3:14); he speaks with him as one friend to another, 'face to face' (Numbers 12:8). He speaks to Israel's heart, like a husband to his wife: 'Therefore, I will now allure her, and bring her into the wilderness, and speak tenderly to her… [and] you will call me "My husband", and no longer will you call me "My Baal"' (Hosea 2:14–16).

Jesus also wants reciprocity. He calls his disciples 'friends' and shares with them everything that the Father has entrusted to him:

'I no longer call you servants, because the servant does not know what his lord does.

I have called you friends because everything I have heard from the Father I have made known to you.

You did not choose me; on the contrary, I chose you,

And I designated you to go and bear fruit and that your fruit should abide,

So that whatever you ask the Father for in my name He will give to you.

This I command you: love one another.' (15:15–17)

Friendship requires a response. Jesus has called us 'friends'. What does he ask so that we may remain such? In reality, he asks nothing for himself. He does not ask us to develop any particular sentiments or to carry out any specific actions toward him, but to love one another: correspondence with his friendship passes through fraternal love. Jesus wants us to love him, concretely, in each one of his brothers and sisters. He asks nothing else for us to remain in his friendship. He does not want us to be servants who simply carry out orders. He wants us to be brothers, sisters, friends, children, side by side with him, in loving obedience to the Father. All our attention, therefore, should be focused on 'abiding' in Jesus, dwelling in him as he dwells in and remains in the Father: 'As the Father loved me, I, too, have loved you; abide in my love' (15:9). Nothing is so important. To remain in communion with Jesus and among ourselves, with his Father and our Father: this is the secret of happiness!

THE WOMAN IN LABOUR
OR THE COMMUNITY OF JESUS

The Master consoles and encourages. He even promises to send his disciples a new consoler and defender—the Spirit, the Paraclete (16:7–15). And he speaks of the hour that approaches—his own and that of the community—with the strongly expressive image of a woman in labour:

'When a woman is giving birth she grieves because her hour has come, but when she bears a child she no longer remembers her suffering out of joy that a man has come into the world. So you, too, are in grief now, but I will see you again and your hearts will rejoice, and no one will take your joy from you.' (16:21–23)

In the Bible, labour pains are a metaphor for suffering. But at the same time, the metaphor indicates the meaning of these sufferings and their intrinsic relationship with life. Here, the woman's hour of labour is first of all an interpretative key for the inevitable 'hour' of Christ, of his paschal mystery.[10] It is a memory of the passion and at the same time of joy and hope. The woman-Church cannot be exempted from the 'pains of labour'. Pope John Paul II does not fail to highlight a connection with the woman-mother beneath the cross:

As we contemplate this Mother, whose heart 'a sword has pierced' (cf. Luke 2:35), our thoughts go to all the suffering women in the world, suffering either physically or morally. In this suffering a woman's sensitivity plays a role, even though she often succeeds in resisting suffering better than a man... But the words of the Gospel about the woman who suffers when the time comes for her to give birth to her child, immediately afterward express joy: it is 'the joy that a child is born into the world'. This joy too is referred to the Paschal Mystery, to the joy which is communicated to the Apostles on the day of Christ's Resurrection.[11]

John Paul II continues, 'It is precisely in the face of the 'mighty works of God' that Saint Paul, as a man, feels the need to refer to what is essentially feminine in order to express the truth about his own apostolic service' (no. 22). This aspect maintains its power even in our time. The *hour* of the woman has not yet been fulfilled, as recalled by the image in Revelation 12:1–17.[12] The 'woman' against whom the dragon lashes out is clothed in the sun and crowned with stars; she is regal and powerful, having the moon as her footstool. Nonetheless, she is weak and suffering like any woman about to give birth. This woman is an icon of the Church.

91

She must live her 'hour' amid the travails of history until the new humanity is born, and with it the new creation (see Romans 8: 19–23).

DIALOGUING WITH THE WORD

> Let's imagine ourselves in the upper room, at table with Jesus, in the place of the disciples, at the washing of the feet. How would I react? Will I welcome this embarrassing gesture by the Lord in silence, or will I react like Peter? If only I could realise that Jesus actually wants to wash my feet. What do I tell him?

I slowly listen again to Jesus' words, his farewell discourse, his testament. I underline the expressions that I feel are most directly addressed to my life. I thank Jesus for having travelled the road of love all the way to the end, of having been only and always love, even in regard to the traitorous disciple.

It is the Lord who chose me and loved me first. He considers me his friend and expects me to respond in kind. He does not ask me for particular commitments and sacrifices—not even for special devotions. He asks me only to observe 'his' commandment, that of loving my brothers and sisters as he has loved me. Could it not be that I load myself with many burdens that are not asked of me, and I fail to pay attention to the only thing that he does ask of me?

Jesus asks me to remain in him; he wants to establish permanent communion with me, among us. He wants to bring us within the current of his filial love, to become one with

the Father and with each other. How do I correspond to his plan
of love?

✛

PAUSE TO PONDER

Father, you have given us in Jesus
the supreme model of love,
the Lord who makes himself a servant,
who takes off the garment
that is the symbol of his life,
to wash my feet, the feet of a sinner.
Do not let me remain indifferent
before this voluntary humbling of my Lord!
Give me the courage
to put on the garment of humility
in order to serve, without rhetoric and in all truth,
my sisters and brothers in faith,
and in particular those who are most weak and defenceless.
I ask you, together with Francis of Assisi:
'May the ardent and gentle force of your love,
O Lord, sweep away from my mind
everything beneath the sky,
that I may die for love of your love,
as you deigned to die for love of my love.'[13]

Chapter 9

THE GREAT PRAYER OF JESUS

With no precise topographical setting, but ideally placed at the summit of the farewell address and as a 'bridge' between the upper room and Gethsemane, Jesus' great prayer to the Father, also called 'the priestly prayer',[1] stands out in John 17. Everything Jesus said to and shared with his disciples in the context of the Last Supper (see John 13—16) is gathered, as it were, in this prayerful ascent from the Son to the Father.

The entrance into this prayer is indicated, even before the words begin, with body language and, more specifically, with a gaze: Jesus 'lifted his eyes to Heaven' (v. 1), as though to establish a direct contact with the Father, to whom he entrusts his own destiny and that of his followers. To lift one's eyes to heaven is a biblical gesture that characterises a person at prayer: 'To you I lift up my eyes, O you who are enthroned in the heavens!' (Psalm 123:1). Jesus teaches us to pray with these words, 'Our Father Who art in Heaven' (Matthew 6:9–13).[2]

Let us ask the Holy Spirit to bring us into this great prayer. Let us ask Jesus to help us enter into his own sentiments in total mutual exchange with the Father and in the indescribable joy that flows from his filial relationship. Lord Jesus, help us feel your love for the Church and make us participants in your passion for unity.

A GLANCE AT THE STRUCTURE

Various elements of form and content converge to highlight the structure of John 17, which opens with an introduction (vv. 1–5) in which Jesus asks the Father to glorify him. A central part follows, which is divided into three sections: first, a retrospective look at the mission already carried out (vv. 6–10); second, a request to the Father to guard and consecrate his own in the truth (vv. 11–19); third, a broadened view into a universal prayer that embraces future believers and asks that 'all may be one' (vv. 20–23). Finally, there is a conclusion, where the theme of glory/glorification returns, a theme that Jesus wishes to share with his disciples (vv. 24–26).

Jesus knows that his hour is approaching, the hour of suffering and death, and with immense trust he asks the Father first of all to glorify him. He does not seek glory from human beings, but only the glory that comes from God. He asks the Father to make the glory of his love fully resplendent. The request for glorification implies the resurrection of Jesus, the indispensable condition for fulfilling the supreme mission he received from the Father—that of communicating eternal life to all humanity.

Jesus presents the Father with four requests. Three of these are formulated with imperative verbs: 'glorify' (your Son); 'guard' (or 'keep' those you have given me); 'consecrate' them in the truth. The fourth request is formulated with the verb *erotao*, 'I pray', and has as its object unity: 'that all may be one!'

The articulation of this passage highlights a double perspective: behind and ahead. After the introduction, we note above all a retrospective view of the mission carried out. It is a gaze full of gratitude that admits having received everything from the Father. The insistence on gift and reciprocity is striking. For Jesus, too— as is typical in the Bible—prayer is above all a remembering. The hour has arrived. The present is charged with a fullness, that of the mission accomplished. It is charged with Jesus' joy at having accomplished the work for which the Father sent him into the world. But Jesus also looks ahead; he looks to the future. He entrusts his own future and that of his community to the Father. He prays that all may be one, as he and the Father are one. Jesus speaks as though he is no longer with his own, as though he has already left the world. There is a play on the words 'presence' and 'absence'. The conclusion refers back to the introduction: Jesus prays again for his own glorification and for ours, and he prays for the Church's unity.

Let us read John 17 arranged in a structured format so as to capture more easily the various articulations. I have highlighted with capital letters the six occurrences of the term 'Father' that span the entire prayer. The imperative verbs are indicated by bold italic text; these express the requests Jesus makes to the Father. The reformulation of these verbs is shown in bold roman text. The various occurrences of the verb 'to give' are expressed in small capitals. These express the awareness of the gift. Some key words that appear frequently are also shown in italics.

Introduction: Father, glorify Your Son (vv. 1–5)

Jesus said these things,
and then he lifted his eyes up to Heaven and said,

FATHER, the hour has come!
Glorify Your Son
so Your Son may **glorify** You,
just as You GAVE him authority over all flesh,
so You may GIVE *eternal life*
to all those You have GIVEN to him.
Now this is *eternal life*,
to *know* You—the One, True God—
and the one You *sent*, Jesus Christ.
I **glorified** You on earth,
by completing the work You GAVE me to do,
and now, You **glorify** me in Your presence, FATHER,
with the **glory** I had with You
before the *world* was.

Retrospective view: I have made Your Name known (vv. 6–10)

I have made Your *name known*
to those men You GAVE me from the *world*.
They were Yours and You GAVE them to me,
and they have **kept** Your word.
Now they *know* that
everything You have GIVEN me
is from You,
because I have given them the words
You GAVE me
and they received them,
and they truly *know* that I came from You,
and they believe that You *sent* me.
I am *praying* for them;
I am *praying*, not for the *world*,
but for those You have GIVEN me,
Because they are Yours,
and everything of mine is Yours,
and Yours is mine,
and I am **glorified** in them.

Future view: Holy Father, keep them… make them holy (vv. 11–19)

Yet I am no longer in the *world*;
and they *are in the world*, and *I am coming to You*.
Holy FATHER, *keep* them in Your *name*,
which You have GIVEN me
that they *may be one*, as We *are one*.

When I was with them, I **kept** them in Your *name*,
which You GAVE me
and **guarded** them,
and none of them was lost

except the son of perdition,
so that Scripture may be fulfilled.
But now *I am coming to You*,
and I am speaking these things in the *world*
that they may have my joy
fulfilled in them.
I have GIVEN them Your word
and the *world* has hated them,
because they are not of the *world*,
just as I am not of the *world*.
I do not *pray* for You to take them out of the *world*,
but for You to *preserve* them from the Evil One.
They are not of the *world*,
just as I am not of the *world*.
Make them holy in the truth;
Your *word* is truth.
Just as You *sent* me into the *world*,
I, too, have *sent* them into the *world*.
And I **consecrate** myself for their sake,
that they may *be made holy* in the truth.

Universal view: that all may be one (vv. 20–23)

But I am *praying* not only for them,
but also for those who believe in me through their word,
so that all *may be one*,
just as You, FATHER, are in me and I in You,
so they, too, may be in Us,
so the *world* may believe that You *sent* me.
And I have GIVEN them the **glory** You GAVE me,
so that they *may be one*
as we *are one*.
I in them and You in me,
so that they may be perfectly *one*,

so that the *world* *may* *know* that You *sent* me
and You *loved* them just as You *loved* me.

Conclusion: an urgent desire or want (vv. 24–26)

FATHER, I desire that they, too, may be with me
where I am—those You GAVE me—
so they may see my **glory**
that You GAVE me,
because You *loved* me before the beginning of the *world*.

Righteous FATHER, the *world* also does not *know* You,
but I *know* You and these *know* that You *sent* me,
and I made Your *name* *known* to them
and I will *make* it *known*,
that the *love* with which You have *loved* me
may be in them, and I in them.

Let us reread this splendid prayer calmly, pausing on the key words, on the verbs that express Jesus' requests, and above all on the subject of the prayer—the Father—from whom Jesus received everything as gift.

- Father: This is the first word, and it sets the tone of the prayer. It appears six times: twice in the introduction and twice in the conclusion, in the central part where God is called 'Holy Father' (v. 11), and towards the end, 'righteous Father' (v. 25). The entire prayer is therefore addressed to the Father. Behind this Greek term is the echo of the familiar term *Abbà* from the Aramaic language (see Mark 14:36).

- Glorify: This is Jesus' first request. The verb 'to glorify' (*doxázo*) recurs four times in the introduction in a chiastic pattern, where the first and the last occurrences are in the imperative: 'glorify' (v. 1) and 'glorify me' (v. 5). The substantive 'glory' (*doxá*) is strictly connected with and specifies the verb (v. 5). The request for glorification is aimed at glorifying the Father. Jesus affirms that he has given the believers the glory that he received from the Father (v. 22), and that he wants them to be with him to contemplate his glory (v. 24). The theme of glory, therefore, unites the beginning and the conclusion of this great prayer.

- **Eternal life:** Woven in with the theme of glory is that of 'life' (vv. 2–3), which is strictly connected with his mission as the good shepherd: 'I have come that you might have life and have it abundantly' (John 10:10). He is already communicating a life that lasts eternally, different from that which is born and dies, like the frailness of 'flesh'. Of what does this life consist? He describes this later on in the prayer when he states that to live is 'to know' the one true God and the One he sent (v. 3). It means remaining and being consecrated in the Word, which is truth (v. 17). Further, it means experiencing the ineffable divine love, that same love with which the Son feels loved by the Father (vv. 23–25). The Spirit—that is, Love—is the principle of this new and definitive life.

- **You gave me:** This prayer surprises us with the frequent repetition of the verb 'to give' (*didômi*). It occurs 15 times, but rarely is it found twice in the same verse (vv. 2, 6, 8, 24). In the eyes of the Son, everything appears as a gift coming from the Father, a gift that is to be communicated to the brothers and sisters. The greatest gifts that the Father offers the Son are in fact 'men' (*anthropoi*), the human persons (men and women) that Jesus has the power to make divine, communicating to them eternal, divine life. Jesus perceives his entire mission as gift: it is the work that the Father gave him to carry out (v. 4); he manifested his Name and gave his Word/s (vv. 8–14). He prayed for those the Father gave him (vv. 9–12), that they be given his same glory (v. 22). He wants this gift to last for ever (v. 24). As in his cry of jubilation (Matthew 11:27; Luke 10:21), here too Jesus appears as the Son who has received everything from his Father and wants to retain nothing for himself. Rather, he desires to communicate everything to the believers 'that they may have my joy fulfilled in them' (John 17:13).

- **To know:** Life ultimately consists in knowing God. It is not a matter of merely intellectual knowledge but rather affective, experiential, relational knowledge. To know God as Father is necessarily a relational fact. 'Father' speaks of relationship; it is a relational term. The only ones who can know God as Father are those who conduct themselves as children, those who enter into a vital relationship with him, just like his Son, Jesus. In this sense, to know is already to love; in fact, it is entirely a question of love. The good shepherd introduces his sheep into the same loving knowledge that exists between him and the Father (John 10:14–15).

- **Guard (or keep) them:** This is Jesus' second request to the Father, formulated first as an imperative. 'Guardian' or 'keeper' (Hebrew: *shomer*) is a very dear title in the Bible. God is the keeper of Israel, the guardian who 'never sleeps' (Psalm 121:4). He keeps vigil and protects his people like a shepherd guards his sheep. This was Jesus' duty as long as he was in the world. He has no intention of failing in his role as shepherd and guardian, but now he is approaching death and intends to defend his own by entrusting them directly to the Father in whom all his trust rests. 'Protect me, O God, for in you I take refuge,' Psalm 16:1 says. Jesus prays, 'Holy Father, keep them in Your name.' He does not ask that believers be removed or spared from the adversities connected with living in the world, but that the Father keep them from evil, or, better, from the Evil One. This echoes the final invocation of the Lord's Prayer: 'deliver us from evil' (Matthew 6:13).

- **Name**: In the Bible, a name indicates the person in his uniqueness. Thus, 'the communication of the name of God means the manifestation of God himself'.[3] This is not to say that God was not already known to Israel, but that Jesus revealed him as Father. In this sense, he fulfilled Psalm 22:22: 'I will tell of your name to my brothers and sisters,' and Isaiah 52:6: 'Therefore my people shall know my name; therefore in that day they shall know that it is I who speak; here am I.' Jesus made the divine name knowable, like a radical 'here I am', a reliable presence: God is Father. Jesus is the epiphany of the Father; those who see him see the Father (John 14:9). All those God 'gave' (*hous edokas*) to him became the consignees of the revelation that Jesus made of the Name, that is, of the paternal face of God. The community of believers recognises itself above all as a 'gift of God'.

- **Make them holy**: This is the third request of Jesus. The verb *hagiázo* (sanctify/consecrate) brings us into the area of biblical Judaic tradition. Consecration was carried out using a special oil. An oil for sacred anointing (*shemen mishchat-kodesh*) was prepared with a mixture of olive oil and precious balsams (see Exodus 30:22–35). However, at the origin of every consecration is the Spirit, as is clear from Isaiah 61:1—'The spirit of the Lord God is upon me, because the Lord has anointed me; he has sent me to bring good news'—a text that Jesus applied to himself in Luke 4:18. Jesus is the Christ, that is, the Anointed One, the Consecrated One. He has a clear awareness of being sanctified/ consecrated by the Father (John 10:36). Here he asks the Father to consecrate/make holy those whom the Father gave him: his Church. He declares that he consecrates himself for our love in such a way that we, too, can be consecrated, made holy in the truth. It is too little to understand this expression in an ethical sense. The consecration Jesus speaks of is tantamount to the gift of his own life, the supreme offering/sacrifice of love.

- **Truth**: We know from the prologue that 'grace and truth' (*cháris kaì aletheia*) 'came through Jesus Christ' (John 1:17). He is the way, the truth, and the life (John 14:6). The word of the Father is truth, and this word became flesh in Jesus Christ. In this sense, truth is 'the evidence of well-tried life'.[4] It is in this Truth, which speaks of all the faithful love of the Father, that believers are consecrated. Where there are charity and truth, there is the Spirit who christifies.

- **World**: The frequency of the word 'world' in this prayer is surprising: it occurs 18 times! The first and last of these instances carry us beyond the present dimension: 'before the world was' (v. 5); 'before the beginning of the world' (v. 24). The world is the great receiver of the love of the Father (John 3:16) and, in that sense, of the mission of Jesus and his community. To be 'in the world' is the constitutive dimension of the human person, the dimension fully assumed by the incarnate Word (John 1:1– 18). But in Johannine language, 'world' is an ambiguous term. It describes in a negative way the shadowy reality that contrasts with the light. It is the dominion of the Evil One, the prince of this world. Jesus does not and could not pray for the world understood in this sense: that would be to pray against himself and his own mission. He was sent into the world to liberate from the world, meaning from the negativity, the dominion and the arrogance that characterise the logic of the world. His disciples and his Church remain in the world but are not of the world, and must not be such in any way. They have been sent into the world as Jesus was. The final word is love, also and especially for this world: the unity of believers must shine as a bright sign so that the world may believe and embrace love.

- **I pray**: The last request is introduced with particular care, with the verb *erotao*, which characterises the prayer of petition and intercession. The same verb is used to express the intercession of Jesus before his Father so that he might send another Paraclete (John 14:16). In the context of John 17, this occurs three times: twice in verse 9 in the antithetic form (I am praying for them/ I am not praying for the world) and a third time in verse 20, where the subjects of Jesus' prayer are the future believers. Jesus is certain that his work will have a future; in fact, he also prays for those who will believe in him through the preaching and witness of his disciples.

• **Oneness/Unity**: What Jesus asks for and greatly desires for his Church in every age is unity: that his believers might form one community, that they may be one, as he is with the Father. The model for unity among believers is the same unity/communion that exists between the Father and Jesus, based on intimate knowledge and love. The unity of believers among themselves and with Jesus is the indispensable condition for being in union with the Father and for witnessing his love to the world, 'so the world may believe' (John 17:21).

We have underscored some key words. Now we will seek to reread the text as a whole, pausing to gaze contemplatively on the various scenes that compose this sublime prayer.

1. 'FATHER, GLORIFY YOUR SON'

How daring the Lord Jesus is in his prayer! His first request is to advance the plea for his glorification. He knows he can do this; even more, he feels the necessity to do so. His entire life is characterised by the glory of the Father; his food and nourishment are to do his Father's will; his joy, to communicate his love. Jesus knows that the supreme trial awaits him: the betrayal and abandonment by his own, false accusations, condemnation, beatings, torture, and finally death. Yet he speaks of glory. He knows his Father will not abandon him to the power of death. To be glorified in the resurrection is the condition for communicating eternal truth and thus fully glorifying the Father by completing his project.

2. 'I HAVE MADE YOUR NAME KNOWN'

Reflecting with a quick look at the mission carried out, Jesus could say, 'I have made known (*ephanérosá*) Your Name.' He was the revealer of the Father, his epiphany. 'Whoever has seen me has seen the Father,' he said to Philip (John 14:9). The Church was born on the basis of this revelation—born as a welcoming embrace of the word of the Father, communicated by Jesus. Welcoming the Word creates a knowledge that becomes experience; it creates community of life: 'they know that everything You have given me is from You, because I have given them the words You gave me, and they received them' (17:7–8). Here again, Jesus takes up in a prayerful manner the theme developed in the first part of the farewell discourse, specifically in John 14:15–24, on the need for remaining in the word and on love as the guardian/observer of his commandments. And his commandment is fraternal love. His disciples welcome this word, and thus they know—with intimate and personal knowledge—that it is truthful and worthy of faith: 'they believe' (*epísteusan*: 17:8). 'The certainty of faith is not founded on external witness, but on the experience of life communicated by practising the message of Jesus which creates communion with him.'[5]

3. 'HOLY FATHER, KEEP THEM'

Here Jesus speaks as one outside the scene—no longer in the world. In a certain sense, he is living this prayer in an attitude of detachment from his own—presence in absence. He turns to the Father, calling him 'holy', in total accord with the religious tradition of his people. In fact, the Bible refers to God as the Holy One par excellence, as three times holy. Sanctity and glory go together and speak of the transcendence, the splendour and the total otherness of God.

What does Jesus ask of the Holy Father? To keep those the Father gave him, his community. He has absolutely no intention of abandoning his own even in death. Thus he entrusts them directly to the care of the Father, which will be carried out in a project of communion. The scope of the safeguarding of the Father is in fact the unity of the group: 'that they may be one as we are one'. This unity has as its model the unity between the Father and the Son. 'The Father and I are one,' Jesus says in John 10:30.

Jesus asks for his community 'fullness of joy', his own joy. This eruption of joy is striking at such a dramatic moment, and it is undoubtedly the sign of a climax. Jesus is going to the Father: 'I am coming to You' (vv. 11, 13). How could he not be joyful? He speaks of joy to his disciples in his farewell address while never separating affliction from joy. The present moment is like that of a woman who is suffering the pains of birth. But her sorrow carries in its womb the joy of life and is not distinguished from it (see John 16:21–24). In the background we can hear an echo of the psalms of ascension, so vibrant with joy. They echo the joy of the pilgrim who is climbing towards the temple, the place of divine presence: 'I was glad when they said to me, "Let us go to the house of the Lord!"' (Psalm 122:1). Jesus is about to ascend to his Father, and Jesus desires that we might possess the fullness of his joy.

Jesus keeps the polarities of joy and struggle together. He does not ask that his community be spared the adversities of the world: he does not desire a disincarnated Church. The Son was sent by the Father for love of the world, and he sends his disciples into the world in the same way: full of love for this world, but free and pure with respect to the logic of the world. Insofar as they are in the world, they are exposed to the attacks of the Evil One. But they need never fear, because Jesus has conquered 'the ruler of this world' (John 12:31), and he intercedes for them before the Father.

Jesus knows that he is going to his death. He wants to live this event as the supreme offering of love. Verse 19 undoubtedly marks a climax: 'I consecrate myself for their sake that they may be made holy in truth.' This expression is pregnant with meaning. It indicates Christ's total dedication to his mission, to the point of sacrificing his own life. It is the reason this prayer is called 'priestly'.

4. 'THAT THEY MAY BE ONE!'

The last request of Jesus to the Father expresses his greatest and most passionate desire: the unity of all in love. It is the reason why the Father sent him into the world and why Jesus goes to his death. Caiaphas, in his role as high priest, prophetically announces the decree of condemnation: 'He prophesied that Jesus would die for the nation, and not only for the nation but also so that the scattered children of God might gather into one' (John 11:51–52). Jesus the good shepherd affirms that he has 'other sheep' who are not of the fold of Israel and who will also form 'one flock' (John 10:16). Behold the mission of Jesus: to unite his brothers and sisters, the family of God, the scattered children, 'so that all may be one!'

In John 17, the theme of unity is introduced with verse 11. It is taken up again and developed in verses 21–23, according to the typical procedure of the fourth evangelist. The expression 'one' (hen) is used five times, with a concentration of four occurrences in verses 21–23. Let us pay particular attention to the construction of verse 21, which is composed of two parallel phrases. Each of them is introduced by the conjunction hína (so that/in order that), indicating the goal or end:

so that [hína] all may be one;
just as You, Father, are in me
and I in You,

so they, too, may be in Us,
so [*hína*] the world may believe that You sent me.

Jesus asks that Christians may be one, as he is one with the Father. Obviously this means a profound unity, one that goes far beyond visible and organisational aspects. Certainly visibility is also necessary so that the world may believe. But visible unity is, properly speaking, a manifestation of a profound and vital reality, such as binds the branches and the vine (John 15:1–5). All/one: a vital tension in the dynamic of love that does not suppress differences. It values the uniqueness of persons. The model of this marvellous creation of love is the Holy Trinity, the unity of the Father and the Son in the vital communion of the same Spirit. A unity of distinct Persons, a unity in Love.

The unity of believers—all one—is the fundamental presupposition in order that 'the world may believe'. Let us note how the first goal (*hína*, 'so that') tends decisively toward the second, that is, the mission: so that the world may believe and thus become participants in the saving project of the Father who so loved the world 'that He gave His only begotten Son' (John 3:16). 'The unity of the Church, like the mutual love of the believers (see 13:35), continues the revelation of Christ in the world and places men and women before the urgency of believing.'[6]

Jesus' prayer gathers the Church in every age, as gift and responsibility. In his encyclical *Ut Unum Sint*, John Paul II writes:

The Catholic Church acknowledges and confesses the weaknesses of her members, *conscious that their sins are so many betrayals of and obstacles to the accomplishment of the Saviour's plan. Because she feels herself constantly called to be renewed in the spirit of the Gospel, she does not cease to do penance. At the same time, she acknowledges and exalts still more* the power of the Lord, *who fills her with the gift of holiness, leads her forward, and conforms her to his Passion and Resurrection... 'The Church is not a reality closed in on herself. Rather, she is permanently open to missionary and ecumenical endeavour, for she is sent to the world to announce and witness, to make present and spread the mystery of communion which is essential to her...' God wills the Church, because he wills unity, and unity is an expression of the whole depth of his agape.*[7]

Even in the midst of contradictions and many tensions, our times are witnessing a growing thirst for unity, a strong need for communion. The Spirit continues to breathe on our troubled world, raising up prophets of communion, men and women who dedicate their lives to unity.

'That all may be one!' Chiara Lubich, founder of the Focolare movement, declared, 'We were born through these words.' Her goal was to bring about unity in the world.

Unity is our specific vocation. Unity is the word that synthesises our spirituality. Unity, which for us encompasses every other supernatural reality, every other practice or commandment, every other religious attitude.[8]

Father James Alberione, the founder of the Pauline Family, was also a prophet of unity, centred in communicating Jesus as Way, Truth and Life (see John 14:6), the Master with the meek heart who attracted all to himself (Matthew 11:28). Alberione proposed praying daily the priestly prayer (John 17), the great prayer of Jesus for unity, in the context of eucharistic adoration.

DIALOGUING WITH THE WORD

Let us enter into dialogue with Jesus, making his prayer our own. The first Christians lived the exciting experience of meeting God as the trustworthy Father of Jesus Christ. In the letters of Paul and Peter, we find three hymns of benediction that begin with the same words: 'Blessed be the God and Father of our Lord Jesus Christ' (2 Corinthians 1:3; Ephesians 1:3; 1 Peter 1:3).

How do I live in filial relationship with the Father? What does being sons and daughters of the Father imply? Am I grateful for all God continually offers and gives me?

Jesus lives in joy because he lives in love, in full communion with the Father and with his own people. Joy flows from love and must be shared in order to be total. Jesus desires that this same joy might dwell in us, that nothing will disturb this joy, that no one will take it away from us. He desires that heaven may already exist here and now: in our hearts filled with his joy!

'They were Yours and You gave them to me,' Jesus said. We, too, can say this about our loved ones, especially our brothers and sisters in faith. Community is given to us as a gift even before it is a commitment and call to responsibility. Do I live my fraternal relationships as a gift?

How do I embrace Jesus' prayer for unity? How much do I let my heart be touched by his passion for unity? Does his ardent desire burn in me: 'that all may be one'? How do I participate in bringing about this divine project?

The apostle Paul made his own the passion of Christ for unity. He invites us to maintain 'the unity of the spirit in the bond of peace. One Lord, one faith, one baptism, one God and Father of us all' (Ephesians 4:3–6). Am I a person of peace and communion? Do I pray to grow always more in these attitudes?

PAUSE TO PONDER

Jesus, how much love you reveal to us as you draw near to your passion; how much love you communicate in your prayer to the Father, the highpoint of your farewell address! Thank you, Lord Jesus, for your prayer. Thank you because you desire that all may be one with you and your Father in the Spirit of Love.

To enter into the prayer of Jesus is to encounter love in action; it is to encounter Love who speaks to the loved one with the clear and grateful gaze of the Son. He welcomes everything as a gift of love.

Let us pause to reflect on the hymn of benediction that opens the letter to the Ephesians (1:3–14), thanking the Father who has called us to be holy and blameless, true sons and daughters in his Son, Jesus. Let us pray:

Holy Father,
hear the prayer of your Son, Jesus:
grant that we may all be one in Love,
in the living communion
of your Holy Spirit.

Make us persons of communion
and of peace.
Let your face shine on us
and keep us in your name.

Teach us
to let ourselves be guarded by you,
to let ourselves be gathered in your embrace.
Never permit us to depart from
your Fatherly embrace.

Bind us together
like many grains in one ear of wheat,
like one cluster of grapes,
like one entity in your Son, Jesus.

✳

Chapter 10

THE CRUCIFIED KING

The beginning of John 18 signals a change of scene: after his intense prayer (ch. 17), Jesus leaves Jerusalem with his disciples, crosses the Kidron Valley and withdraws to a 'garden'. The story of his passion begins (chs. 18—19). Events start moving faster, but Jesus is not overwhelmed: instead, he reveals himself as Lord. His intimate relationship with the Father confers upon him that extraordinary energy of love that carries him onward until the 'All has been fulfilled!' (*consummatum est*).

In terms of time, the sequence of events occupies less than an entire day, the day of preparation for the feast of Passover (*Pesach*).[1] The time indications that are provided allow us to subdivide the account into three main portions:

- The first (18:1–27) takes place during the night. It describes the arrest of Jesus, his interrogation before Annas, and Simon Peter's denials.
- The second (18:28–19:16) unfolds from early morning to midday. The setting moves back and forth between the praetorium of Pilate and outside the praetorium, where Jesus' accusers are, and it concludes with his condemnation to death on the cross.
- The third (19:17–42) recounts the great scene of Golgotha up to the burial of Jesus, before sunset, when the Passover begins.

Within the framework of these temporal divisions, various scenes take place that we will now consider in greater depth. Let us allow ourselves to be drawn into the action by the various characters and, above all, by the attitude of Jesus. Let us contemplate the Man of Sorrows, the Son of Man raised upon the cross, our King.

IN THE GARDEN: LOVE BETRAYED

The place that Jesus chooses for the dialogue with his Father is an orchard/garden on the other side of the Kidron Valley, at the base of the Mount of Olives. From the first two Gospels, we also learn the name of the place, 'Gethsemane'.[2] With subtle allusion to the garden of Eden, where the life and history of sinful humanity began, John speaks of a *kepos*, a garden (18:1). He uses the same term for the place of burial (19:41). Judas also knows that garden, which Jesus treasures as a place of prayer, and goes there with the soldiers and guards sent by the high priest.

John highlights the mastery with which Jesus goes to meet his destiny. If he had wanted to, he could have fled. In about ten minutes, he could have been over the Mount of Olives and heading into the desert, leaving his pursuers behind. But he does not do that. This is his 'hour', the hour established by the Father. It is not Judas who has the leading role, but Jesus. He is the one who 'betrays' himself, or rather 'hands himself over'.[3] Fully aware of what is going to happen, he goes out to meet his destiny:

Jesus, knowing all that was to befall him, came out and said to them, 'Who are you looking for?' They answered him, 'Jesus of Nazareth!' He said to them, 'I am he!' Now Judas, who handed him over, was also standing with them. When Jesus said to them, 'I am he!' they drew back and fell to the ground. (18:4–6)

In the darkness, a light shines forth: I AM! Its effect 'demonstrates that we are witnessing something that is more than a simple self-identification. It echoes the 'I am' of the God of the biblical tradition, who is identified with Jesus as he goes to his passion.'[4] According to the synoptic Gospels, at the arrest of Jesus all the disciples abandon him and flee. But in John, Jesus himself enables them to leave freely. The good shepherd defends his flock, and he saves the life of his followers by handing over his own: 'If you are looking for me, let these others go,' so what he said might be fulfilled: 'I lost none of those You gave to me' (vv. 8–9).

Simon Peter intervenes. He takes the initiative of armed defence, pulling out his sword and striking. He cuts off the right ear of Malchus, a slave of the high priest.[5] And he may have done even more had the Master not stopped him: 'Put the sword in its scabbard. Am I not to drink from the cup my Father has given me?' (v. 11). This is the method of Jesus!

THE COURTYARD OF THE HIGH PRIEST: LOVE DENIED

Jesus is therefore arrested and brought first of all to Annas, the former high priest, who is the father-in-law of Caiaphas. Jesus is not brought directly to Caiaphas, the high priest currently in office, but rather to his father-in-law. This fact could imply that Annas was the one who ordered the arrest. He must have been highly influential.

The interrogation takes place at night, and it clearly bears the marks of darkness: violence, lying, abuse of power, and betrayal, precisely on the part of the disciple who had declared that he was ready to give his life for his Master. After lying to the gatekeeper (v. 17), Peter warms himself at the fire in the company of the guards while Jesus is put on trial:

So the high priest questioned Jesus about his disciples and about his teaching. Jesus answered him, 'I have spoken openly to the world; I have always taught in a synagogue or in the Temple'— where all the Jews gather—'and I have said nothing in secret. Why are you questioning me? Ask those who heard what I said to them. After all, they know what I said.' When he said these things one of the attendants who was standing by gave Jesus a slap and said, 'Is that how you answer the high priest?' Jesus answered him, 'If I have spoken wrongly, bear witness against the wrong, but if I have spoken rightly, why do you hit me?' (vv. 19–23)

Jesus does not refuse to be questioned, but he objects to the manner in which this is done. He has taught openly, in public places, in the synagogues and the temple: 'Ask those who heard what I said.' This frankness costs him a violent blow from one of the guards, who may have been looking for a promotion. How does the Master react? He does not offer the other cheek (see Matthew 5:39); nevertheless, he behaves as he has taught. Even more, he helps us understand what it means, beyond the metaphor, to turn the other cheek. There is no victimhood on the part of Jesus. I imagine that he looked into the eyes of that violent guard and replied to him in a calm but firm voice. His reply appeals to reason: 'If I have spoken wrongly, bear witness against the wrong.' It is a lesson on true freedom based on discernment. How often we become the slaves of violence, perhaps in order to make a good impression before some influential person. The look from Jesus and his words invite us never to delegate reason, never to delegate our own capacity to reflect and act in consequence: 'If I have spoken rightly, why do you hit me?'

Jesus' question brings silence. Brought back to reason, the guard who struck him does not answer, but Annas is also silent. So Jesus is brought to Caiaphas, who has already decided to have him put to death: 'You do not know anything!' he said to the Sanhedrin. 'Do you not realise that it is better for one man to die than to have the whole nation be destroyed?' (John 11:49–50; see 18:14).

Meanwhile, beside the fire, Simon Peter is carrying out his denial. After the doubt raised by the gatekeeper, more suspicions are added by the servants and soldiers standing together with him around the fire:

Now Simon Peter was standing there warming himself. So they said to him, 'Are not you one of his disciples, too?' He denied it and said, 'I am not.' One of the servants of the high priest, a kinsman of the one whose ear Peter had cut off, said, 'Did I not see you with him in the garden?' Again Peter denied it, and at once a cock crowed. (18:25–27)

That cockcrow in the night brings back to Peter's mind the words of the Master (13:38). How was it possible to disown Love? How was such a rapid and shameful capitulation possible? Where is the Peter who cut off the ear of Malchus, the Peter who was so sure of giving his life?

IN THE PRAETORIUM: LOVE INSULTED

Early in the morning, Jesus is brought before the Roman authorities in the praetorium that Pilate occupies. But this is the preparation day for the Passover, and the Passover lamb has to be eaten in full observance of the Law. For this reason, Jesus' accusers remain outside the building where the pagans reside. The accusers do not want to be contaminated.

So Pilate then comes out to them. The evangelist does not use even a single word to introduce Pilate, presuming that all Gospel readers will know who he is.[6] The conversation between Pilate and the Jewish authorities demonstrates their mutual embarrassment. Because there was no evidence against Jesus, the very fact of his being handed over has to act as proof: 'If the fellow were not a wrongdoer we would not have handed him over to you' (18:30).

Pilate then goes back into the praetorium and summons Jesus, who has no concerns about contamination. He is the Lamb who takes upon himself the guilt of all, the sin of the world (John 1:29). Jesus does not refuse to speak with Pilate. It is indeed striking how much space John devotes to this scene: almost 30 verses to narrate some facts that are certainly fundamental; none of the other evangelists recounts the scene at such great length. In particular, the impression is that John is marking out the rhythm of his narrative through the coming and going of Pilate. Let's take an overall look at these movements:

- 18:29: Pilate *comes out* of the praetorium to speak with the Jews.
- Verse 33: He *goes back into* the praetorium and talks with Jesus (the question about the kingdom).
- Verse 38: He again *goes out* to speak with the Jews (the choice between Jesus and Barabbas).
- 19:1: Pilate has Jesus scourged (it is implied that he *goes back in*).
- Verse 4: He *goes out* and presents Jesus, saying: 'Look at the man.'
- Verse 9: He *goes back in* to interrogate Jesus again.
- Verse 13: He *comes back out* for the fourth time, and pronounces the condemnation of Jesus.

At the basis of this going out and coming back in is that part of the audience takes place inside the building, and part outside, out of respect for the Jews who could not enter the home of a pagan, to avoid becoming ritually impure. But one can also recognise here a stylistic-theological elaboration typical of the evangelist. Following the action from start to finish, seven distinct but closely connected scenes are set out, so that the entire episode presents an ascending development culminating in the seventh scene, when Pilate says, 'Here is your king!' (19:14). The theme of royalty is particularly close to the heart of the evangelist John.[7]

To Pilate's first question, 'Are you the King of the Jews?' (18:33), Jesus responds with another question: 'Are you saying this on your own or have others told you about me?' (v. 34). As in the previous dialogues with Nicodemus and the Samaritan woman, these questions and Pilate's reaction constitute, in a manner of speaking, the preliminaries. The decisive entry into the topic takes place when Jesus declares that his kingdom is of a different origin, it is not 'from' (*ek*) this world. This is proven by the fact that he has no army; he has no one fighting in his defence: 'If my Kingdom were of this world my attendants would fight so that I wouldn't be handed over to the Jews, but as it is my Kingdom is not from here' (v. 36).

Pilate continues pressing his question, more eager to come up with an accusation than to follow a subtle line of reasoning: 'So you *are* a king?' (v. 37). It's as if he is saying, 'Stick with the question, don't get fancy.' Jesus doesn't disappoint him: '*You* say that I am a king. For this I was born and for this I came into the world—to bear witness to the truth. Everyone who is of the truth hears my voice' (v. 38).

Astonishing. This is the same Jesus who had fled all alone after the multiplication of the loaves, when the people wanted to take him away to make him king (6:15). Now that he has been bound and handed over to the Romans by the leaders of his people, he openly affirms his royalty. He is not only a king, he is fully aware of being one. He has come into the world to be king, and to bear witness to the truth. The truth is a crucial question, and the basis of any respectable trial. 'What is truth?' Pilate asks. But he does not wait for a reply.

The king who does not covet power, who does not flaunt the signs and wonders that have accompanied his words, who does not coerce anyone, remains alone. The echo of Pilate's question fades into the silence of the praetorium, but it would continue to resound through history. 'What is truth?' Jesus had confided to his friends at supper the evening before: 'I am the truth.' Not in an abstract and doctrinal form, but the truth (*aletheia*) in person, the truth to be followed, the way that leads to life. But instead of Jesus they prefer Barabbas,[8] a murderous brigand.

'BEHOLD THE MAN! BEHOLD YOUR KING!'

Jesus is the king who is mocked, humiliated, scorned (John 19:1–3). The head crowned with thorns drips blood down a face disfigured by blows. But from his mouth comes no curse, no threat of vengeance: 'When he was reviled he did not reply in kind' (1 Peter 2:23).[9] He is truly Lord amid so much violence and brutality.

In the following scene, Pilate goes out to the Jews for the third time, saying: 'Look, I am bringing him out to you so you will know that I find no case against him' (John 19:4). But the next verse shows that Jesus is not at all brought out by Pilate. He comes out on his own, as befits a true king: 'So Jesus came outside, wearing the crown of thorns and the purple robe.'

Pilate immortalises him in three words: 'Look at the man!' (*idoù ho anthrepos*, v. 5).

The scene speaks for itself. Just three words suffice, words that are certainly not full of compassion on the part of Pilate, but rather of mockery and disdain towards both the accusers and the accused. Behold the man that you want to eliminate! But John means much more by these three words. They are a dazzling illumination of the proclamation of the prophets. They evoke the Man of Sorrows spoken of in Isaiah 53, and at the same time the mysterious Son of Man of the nocturnal visions of Daniel. This Son of Man receives glory and the power to judge all the kings of the earth (Daniel 7:13–14). He is truly the Man who represents all of the humiliated and persecuted, the Man without deceit or hypocrisy, totally open to love. Behold the Man, the image of God!

Pilate knows only the gods created by men, while here before him is the Son of God. Now fear invades his soul. 'Where are you from?' he asks Jesus, after going back into the praetorium for the third time. But he has not yet entered within himself, so he obtains no reply.

The scene draws near its conclusion. Pilate is incapable of opposing the crowd, and he fears enmity with Caesar. He can do nothing but pronounce the condemnation. But before this, he again takes his time mocking the accused and his accusers. The scene is particularly solemn. The evangelist is careful to relate the details: we are outdoors, in a place that must have been well-known and visible, called the *Lithóstrotos* in Greek, or *Gabbatha* in Hebrew.

John specifies that it was about midday, the sixth hour of the day of preparation for the Passover. At that hour the head of the family would be preparing to take the Passover lamb to the temple to be slaughtered. This coincidence impresses the contemplative John, who is particularly close to the world of the temple. The truth conveyed by this sign of the Passover lamb is about to be fulfilled—and together with that, the truth of the kingdom of God, which Israel experienced in an eminent way in the exodus of liberation from Egypt. God rules differently from man, and God liberates in a different way. It is against this Passover background that John interprets the condemnation of Jesus, preceded by the final display that Pilate made of him: 'Here is your king!' (*íde ho basileùs hymon*).

Here is our King! He wears a crown of thorns and a piece of purple cloth as a cloak. His hands are bound. He doesn't say a word, like a lamb led to the slaughter (see Isaiah 53:7). This really is our King. He does not dominate, but reigns by attracting—irresistibly.

THE GREAT SCENE OF GOLGOTHA

In comparison with the synoptic Gospels, John's narration leads rapidly to Golgotha, where the great scene of the crucifixion takes place. Jesus arrives there carrying the cross by himself. The evangelist does not mention Simon of Cyrene. The passage constitutes a unique sequence in seven images:

1. The crucifixion 19:17–18
2. The inscription on the cross ....vv. 19–22
3. The garments and the tunic....................................vv. 23–24
4. The mother and the beloved disciple ....vv. 25–27
5. Thirst and death..vv. 28–30
6. The piercing of the side ....vv. 31–34
7. The testimony of the one who has seen ....vv. 35–37

With our minds illumined by John, let us contemplate the summit of the entire account, the raising up of the Man who draws us from the cross. Let us read the text slowly, dwelling with the eyes of our hearts on the various moments of this great scene of Golgotha.

1. The crucifixion

So they took Jesus in charge. And carrying the cross himself he went out to what was called 'the Place of the Skull', in Hebrew, Golgotha, where they crucified him and with him two others, on either side, while Jesus was in the middle. (John 19:17–18)

Exhausted by a night of torture, Jesus arrives at the place of capital punishment carrying the transversal beam of the cross alone. The place is a spur of rock outside the city walls. It is called the 'Place of the Skull' because of its strange shape, and perhaps because it is the place where the Romans carried out the atrocious punishments reserved for criminals and rebels. That day before the Passover, three men are to be executed in the Place of the Skull. John reports no dialogue between Jesus and the other two men, but he does highlight one detail: the centrality of Jesus' cross. The other two men are crucified 'on either side, while Jesus was in the middle'. This detail reflects the theme of royalty, the subject of the long dialogue with Pilate, and is elaborated in the following scene.

2. The inscription on the cross

Now Pilate wrote a notice and had it placed on the cross, but it was written, 'Jesus of Nazareth, the King of the Jews'. Many of the Jews read this notice, because the place where Jesus was crucified was near the city, and it was written in Hebrew, Latin, and Greek. So the chief priests of the Jews said to Pilate, 'Do not write "The King of the Jews" but instead, "He said, I am the King of the

Jews."' Pilate answered, 'What I have written I have written!' (vv. 19–22)

Pilate plays his role to the very end: he has a *titulus crucis* written— that is, a plaque placed on the cross that displays the reason for the condemnation. He couldn't have found a better way to get his point across. The inscription, in fact, is in three languages: the local language (Hebrew), that of the ruling power (Latin) and the international language of culture and commerce (Greek). It seems that he is mocking the Jews, but in reality he is obeying a mysterious design of divine revelation. The inscription leads to an argument. The chief priests uselessly demand a correction from Pilate. 'The result is that the crucifixion, instead of being a place of profound silence, becomes a scene of preaching.'[10] It is the universal proclamation of the royalty of Christ, of his authentically messianic character. What Pilate has written is up there, above the cross, and remains written for ever.

3. The garments and the tunic

When the soldiers had crucified Jesus they took his cloak and made four parts, one for each soldier, plus the tunic. Now the tunic was seamless, woven from the top in one piece. So they said to each other, 'Let's not tear it; let's draw lots for it instead,' so the Scripture would be fulfilled which said, *They divided my garments among them, and for my clothing they cast lots.* So the soldiers did these things. (John 19:23–24)

John is silent on the mockery of the crucified as recounted by the synoptics.[11] His attention is focused on highly symbolic details. First he gives great attention to the inscription on the cross, in keeping with the central theme of the royalty of Jesus. The next image he presents concerns the division of Jesus' garments by the soldiers. John specifically mentions the tunic, which is not torn but apportioned by the choosing of lots. With his contemplative gaze, the evangelist sees an important symbolic value as shown by the fact that he refers to the scriptures and their fulfilment.[12]

The Fathers of the Church love to see in this seamless tunic, not torn by the soldiers, an image of the Church of Christ and a symbol of the unity for which he prayed and offered himself, 'so that they might be one' (John 17).

4. The mother and the beloved disciple

Now standing by Jesus' cross were his mother and his mother's sister, Mary the wife of Clopas, and Mary Magdalen. When Jesus saw his mother and the disciple he loved standing by he said to his mother, 'Woman, here is your son.' Then he said to the disciple, 'Here is your mother.' And from that hour the disciple took her into his home. (John 19:25–27)

There she is, at the foot of the cross, the mother who at Cana had anticipated the hour of her son. She does not flee but stays standing there. She cannot speak or even cry. She holds everything inside her heart, to avoid increasing her son's pain. Now it is he, the dying son, who takes the initiative. He speaks nine words in all, including the article. The first five are addressed to his mother: *gýnai, íde ho hyiós sou*, 'Woman, here is your son.' Then he turns to the beloved disciple: *íde he méter sou*, 'Here is your mother.'

Jesus calls his mother 'woman', a title that sounds strange on the lips of the dying son. But it is not strange on the lips of the Messiah who here recapitulates all of history. With her new maternity, Mary corresponds to and recalls the first woman, Eve, 'the mother of all living' (Genesis 3:20). The expression 'here is your son' occurs with the corresponding 'here is your mother'. These words establish a new relationship between Mary and the community of believers, represented by the beloved disciple. This time, it is not an angel, but the dying Son himself who proclaims Mary's new maternity.

5. Thirst and death

After this Jesus, knowing that everything had already been accomplished, in order to fulfil the Scripture, said, 'I am thirsty.' There was a container there full of sour wine; so after putting a sponge full of sour wine on some hyssop they held it up to his mouth. When he had taken the sour wine Jesus said, 'All has been fulfilled!' and bowing his head he gave up the spirit. (John 19:28–30)

Seated at the well of Sychar, weary from his journey, at the hottest hour of the day, he had asked the Samaritan woman, 'Give me a drink' (John 4:7). It was the sixth hour, noon-time, the hour of his sentencing to death on the cross. Time seemed to stand still on the cross, and the thirst is excruciating. Jesus has this torture in common with the two men hanging beside him, a searing thirst of fever and death. But this is not the only factor in Jesus' request. John insists upon recalling that Jesus was aware of everything, lucid to the very end. His thirst is part of a larger picture, the immense panorama of the scriptures. It is the thirst for God and for pleasing him. But the response to the thirst of Christ is a sponge soaked in wine vinegar (*óxos*) and hyssop. The evangelist is thinking of Psalm 69:21: 'They gave me poison for food, and for my thirst they gave me vinegar to drink.' Jesus speaks so that the scriptures may be fulfilled, although this does not take anything away from the historical reality of his words. This wine/vinegar alludes to the chalice of the divine will, which Jesus does not refuse. In fact, after drinking the vinegar, he pronounces his last word: *tetélestai*, 'All has been fulfilled!'

What follows is not simply his last breath, but the handing over of his spirit: *parédoken to pnéuma* into the hands of the Father (compare Luke 23:46).

The following two scenes reveal what is unleashed by this total self-donation.

6. The piercing of the side

The Jews, since it was the Day of Preparation and so the bodies wouldn't remain on the crosses—for that Sabbath was a great day—asked Pilate to let them break their legs and take them away. So the soldiers came and they broke the legs of the first one and then of the other who had been crucified with him, but when they came to Jesus and saw that he had already died they did not break his legs, but, instead, one of the soldiers stabbed him in the side with a spear, and at once blood and water came out. (John 19:31–34)

Only John recounts the blow from the lance that pierces the side of the already dead Jesus. This detail should not be included among his tortures, for Christ has already handed over his spirit. Rather, it should be placed in the context of the verification of his death, before handing over his corpse for burial. The evangelist recalls the liturgical historical context: it was the *Parasceve*, the day of preparation for the Passover, which fell on the Sabbath that year. It was therefore the Sabbath par excellence, the *Shabbat Shabbatôn*. In order properly to honour the feast, Pilate grants the application of the *crurifragium*, the hastening of death through the breaking of the legs: otherwise it could take a long time to die from crucifixion.

But in Jesus' case, there is no need to hasten death. For him, everything is already accomplished; he has handed over his spirit. Now even the soldiers realise that he is dead, so there is no need to break his legs. So why the blow from the lance? Why another torment inflicted upon that lacerated body? Why another outrage against the King of the Jews? John does not comment on the reason for this lance blow, but instead concentrates on what it leads to: 'one of the soldiers stabbed him in the side with a spear, and at once blood and water came out' (v. 34).

At first one would not think this unusual. The lance blow releases the liquids found in the human body, half water and the other half blood, according to an ancient Jewish conception. But with his profound vision John sees much more in that pierced side and in what flows from it—blood and water. John sees the fulfilment of the supreme mystery of life. From the pierced side of Jesus flow blood and water, symbols of the gift of life (blood) and of the Spirit (water). These are the symbols of Christian regeneration!

7. The testimony of the one who has seen

And the one who saw it has borne witness and his witness is true, and he knows that he is speaking the truth so you, too, may believe. For these things happened so the Scripture might be fulfilled, *Not a bone of his shall be broken*. And again another Scripture says, *They shall look on him whom they have pierced*. (John 19:35–37)

We are at the last image of the narrative sequence. It does not add any new elements to the scene. But it illuminates the events in a new light, not from the sun or the moon, but from the scriptures that are marvellously fulfilled before the ecstatic gaze of the mystic John. There are two explicit citations, the first from the book of Exodus, the second from the prophet Zechariah.

In Exodus 12:46, we read in regard to the Passover lamb, 'You shall not break any of its bones.' With a slight variation of terminology, the same injunction also occurs in Numbers 9:12. The correspondence between Jesus and the Passover lamb appears clearly. This draws us all the way back to the inaugural words of John the Baptist: 'Here is the Lamb of God who takes away the sin of the world!' (John 1:29). Jesus is the lamb of the Passover liberation.

The second quotation is taken from Zechariah 12:10, in which God says, 'And I will pour out a spirit of compassion and supplication on the house of David and the inhabitants of Jerusalem, so that, when they look on the one whom they have pierced, they shall mourn for him, as one mourns for an only child, and weep bitterly over him, as one weeps over a firstborn.' What is striking about this text is the identification of God with the one who is pierced. The inhabitants of Jerusalem will be able to recognise this mysterious identification only through the Spirit that God will pour over them. This is what John has experienced, and to this he bears witness. And his testimony is true, completely reliable.

DIALOGUING WITH THE WORD

Let us imagine ourselves on Calvary, at the foot of the cross. Let us ask for John's contemplative gaze and the loving heart of the Mother. Let us remain in silence, allowing ourselves to be drawn by Jesus raised up upon the cross.

Let us enter into dialogue with him, our crucified King. Do I truly allow him to reign in my life? How much of his truth inhabits my thoughts, judgments, and feelings? Am I in harmony with the values of my King, with his style of humility and meekness?

What relationship do I have with Mary, given to us as Mother by Jesus on the cross? Can I say, like the beloved disciple, that I have welcomed her into my house? Do I allow her to teach me to withstand trials, to remain standing beneath the cross, fully obedient to the will of the Father?

Let us listen to the yearning of Jesus, to his thirst. What does Christ's thirst prompt within me? How do I respond to his thirst for love? What can I do, personally and as part of a community, for the Man of Sorrows whose passion is prolonged throughout history? Do I recognise the many forms of thirst that afflict those around me?

Let us contemplate the Pierced One, the fountain of divine mercy. Let us thank Christ for the blood and water flowing from his pierced heart, for the gift of the Church, for our rebirth from water and the Spirit.

✝

PAUSE TO PONDER

We sing to you,
the Lamb who was slain,
crucified Love
that regenerates us from the blood
and water flowing from your side.
Praise to you,
Lord Jesus Christ!
We look to you
who reign from the cross,
the Shepherd who has become a Lamb,
an obedient Servant for the sake of love.
Draw us to yourself!
Grant us the grace of following in your footsteps,
of sowing peace where there is bitterness,
of repaying hatred with love,
injury with blessing,
indifference with tenderness,
hostility with gentleness,
evil with goodness.

✳

Chapter 11

MARY MAGDALENE, THE DISCIPLES, AND THOMAS

John 20 recounts the most fascinating news in history: the resurrection of Jesus. This is the direct experience of the first witnesses, the encounter with the living, risen Jesus. An initial panoramic view will help us to distinguish the general characteristics and the pronounced liturgical dimension of this unique account, which is divided into four scenes: the empty tomb and the signs of faith (vv. 1–10), the meeting between Jesus and Mary Magdalene (vv. 11–18), the first appearance of Jesus to the disciples (vv. 19–23), and the second appearance eight days later, with Thomas present (vv. 24–29).

We will dwell especially on the characters of the second and fourth scenes, Mary Magdalene and Thomas, who through contrast are reminiscent of each other: Mary Magdalene is the first to see Jesus, but must refrain from touching him. Thomas, instead, demands to see and touch, and is caught in his own words by the Risen One.

THE FIRST DAY AND EIGHT DAYS LATER

The account of John 20 is divided by three periods of time:

- **Verse 1**: On the first day of the week… in the early morning…
- **Verse 19**: When it was evening of that first day of the week…
- **Verse 26**: And a week later…

Is this a simple indication of time, or is it also liturgical? John seems to weave both dimensions together skilfully. In effect, the appearances of Jesus to the disciples, with Thomas first absent and then present, take place during a gathering that occurs on the evening of the first day of the week and eight days later, respectively. In both cases, therefore, they occur on Sunday.[1]

It is on 'the Lord's Day' (*kyriake heméra* in Greek) that John, exiled to Patmos because of his preaching of the word of God and his witness to Jesus, is caught up in ecstasy (Revelation 1:10). This detail reflects the importance that the first day of the week had acquired within the early Church. In John's perspective, it designates the beginning of the new creation and embraces all of the foundational events of the Christian faith: the resurrection of Jesus, the Easter appearances, the gift of the Holy Spirit.[2]

EARLY IN THE MORNING, IN SEARCH OF THE LORD

A woman, Mary Magdalene, is the first to enter the scene. Unlike in the synoptics, according to which Mary visits the tomb in the company of other women, John leaves out the other female characters and focuses on her. Why only one woman? Why her? The rest of the account will clarify this.

Meanwhile, we should note that 'it was still dark'. Dark outside only or also inside? The two dimensions are interwoven. Mary Magdalene both sees and does not see. She observes but does not understand the meaning. She sees that the great stone has been rolled away from the tomb, but she interprets this as a violation of the tomb. Full of anxiety, she runs to Peter and to the other disciple, and she cries out in desperation: 'They have taken the Lord out of the tomb and we do not know where they have put him!' (John 20:2).

Why does Mary speak in the plural, saying 'We do not know'? Clearly because she was not alone! John does not ignore what is unanimously testified in the entire synoptic tradition. If he leaves out the other characters, it is because he intends to concentrate on this woman, as a symbol of the loving community. But let's continue. How do Peter and the beloved disciple react? The entire scene moves quickly, racing along:

The two of them were running together, but the other disciple ran faster than Peter and came to the tomb first, and when he bent down he saw the linen cloths lying there, but he did not go in. Simon Peter came, too, following him, and he went into the tomb and saw the linen cloths lying there, and the face covering, which had been on his head, was not lying with the linen cloths but was wrapped up separately in its own place. So then the other disciple, who had come to the tomb first, went in, too, and he saw and believed, for they did not yet understand the Scripture that he had to rise from the dead. So the disciples went off home again. (John 20:4–10)

So, running, the beloved disciple arrives at the tomb first. He runs because he loves more, yet he allows Peter to be the first to enter the empty tomb, where they find signs of the risen Jesus. But only of the other disciple is it said that he 'saw and believed'.

Tradition identifies this disciple as John the Evangelist, thus offering an evocative image of two different and yet complementary aspects: the institutional reality of the Church and its charismatic reality.[3] Not everyone can carry out Peter's role, but everyone can recognise himself in the other disciple, who possesses the intuition of love.[4]

IN THE GARDEN: THE RISEN ONE AND MARY

Unlike the two disciples, Mary Magdalene does not return home: she was 'standing near the tomb, weeping outside' (John 20:11).

Mary does not leave the place; she is entirely focused on recovering the mortal remains of her beloved Master. She weeps in sorrow, as the Lord had foretold: 'You will wail and mourn... You will grieve, but your grief will turn to joy' (John 16:20).

The entire sequence sounds strongly allusive. Mary evokes the beloved of the Song of Songs, who seeks her lover until she finds him: 'At night I sought him whom my soul loves... I will seek him whom my soul loves' (Song 3:1–2). And it is in the garden that the beloved encounters her lover after seeking him for so long: 'My beloved has gone down to his garden' (Song 6:2).

The scene recalls the garden of Eden, where the love story between God and humanity began. In John, however, the garden connects the passion and the resurrection: Jesus is betrayed and arrested in a 'garden' (18:1–12), and he is buried in a 'garden' (19:41). The garden in which the passover of Christ's death and resurrection takes place symbolically opens the vast horizons of the new creation.

I would like to note another aspect, concerning Mary Magdalene's body language, specifically the two times she turns from the tomb to the risen Jesus. As we will see, this is a progressive movement of conversion.

Let us imagine the scene: Mary bends towards the tomb. Two angels dressed in white ask her why she is crying, and she responds: 'They have taken my Lord and I do not know where they have put him!' (John 20:13). After saying this, 'she turned around' (estráphe). A man is standing there, but she does not recognise that it is Jesus. She thinks he is the gardener. He asks, 'Woman, why are you weeping? Who are you looking for?' She immediately replies, 'Sir, if you removed him tell me where you put him, and I will take him away' (v. 15). And immediately she turns back towards the tomb (the text does not say this, but it is implied). She cannot keep her eyes from the place where her beloved was laid.

Now something happens that brings about a new movement and a definitive turn, a decisive conversion. 'Jesus said to her, "Mary!"

She turned (*strapheísa*) and said to him, in Hebrew, "Rabboni!" which means, "Teacher!"' (v. 16). As if under a spell, Mary turns towards the one who pronounces her name.[5] She recognises the voice of the Shepherd who calls her by her name and leads her out (see John 10:3). Out from what? Out from mourning and weeping. Out from seeking among the dead the one who is alive.

The garden of mourning becomes the garden of joy; the place of death becomes the place of encounter with the living Jesus. Let us imagine Mary at the feet of Jesus, eagerly embracing him, in a way similar to how Matthew tells the story of the appearance of the risen Jesus to the women: 'They came forward, took hold of his feet, and worshipped him' (Matthew 28:9). Mary must interrupt that embrace (*me mou háptou*; 'do not touch me'), not because the risen Jesus shuns it but because the former physical relationship is no longer possible. A new relationship of faith is required, as will be clarified in the scene with Thomas. Also, there is a mission to be accomplished, a message to be proclaimed: 'But go to my brothers and tell them, "I am ascending to my Father and your Father, and to my God and your God"' (v. 17).

Mary Magdalene is usually presented as the one who announces the resurrection of Jesus. But if we pay attention to the words, we notice that the risen Jesus sends her as the herald of his ascension.[6] This detail indicates the fulfilment of the saving work of Christ: the one who descended now ascends to his Father and ours. We note that only here, for the first time in John, God is called Father of Jesus and our Father on a level of full reciprocity. The possibility of becoming 'sons of God', announced in the prologue (John 1:12), has been realised.[7]

The scene ends with Mary Magdalene carrying out the mission she has received: *heoraka tón Kýrion*, 'I have seen the Lord!' (20:18). The disciples will address the same words to Thomas: 'We have seen the Lord!' (v. 25). This is the essential Easter witness. Mary Magdalene is the first witness to the risen Jesus, 'the apostle of the apostles'.[8]

AT EVENING, WITH THE DOORS LOCKED: THE RISEN JESUS AND THE DISCIPLES

The third scene takes place on the evening of the first day. The characters are the risen Jesus and his disciples, but with a sharp difference of roles: Jesus is the active, speaking character, while the disciples do not say a word. The evangelist notes, however, that they 'rejoiced when they saw the Lord'.

This is the joy of the encounter with the risen Jesus: a spontaneous, unexpected, divine joy. It is the joy of every Sunday, the weekly Easter, if we allow ourselves to be illuminated by the risen Lord. True joy is the fruit of an encounter of love; the love of the risen Jesus who comes near, approaches, walks along the way with us and brings newness to our lives (cf. Luke 24:13–35).[9]

The disciples have gathered in a closed location, locked in by fear. But the closed doors do not prevent the risen Jesus from coming and being in the midst of his own:

When it was evening on that first day of the week, and the doors had been locked where the disciples were for fear of the Jews, Jesus came and stood in their midst and said to them, 'Peace be with you!' And after saying this he showed them his hands and side. The disciples rejoiced when they saw the Lord. He said to them again, 'Peace be with you! As the Father has sent me, I, too, send you.' And after saying this he breathed on them and said, 'Receive the Holy Spirit! Whose sins you forgive, they have already been forgiven; Whose sins you retain, they have already been retained.' (John 20:19–23)

The first word of the risen Jesus is 'peace', the biblical *shalom*. His peace brings complete salvation, accomplished through his sacrifice. Jesus displays his wounds, hands and pierced side. It is not a ghost, it is he, the crucified and risen Lord! This sign of recognition dispels all doubt and allows the disciples to rejoice completely. His wounds are not an accusation, but speak of peace and forgiveness. Jesus grants the disciples to enter into his own mission that he received from the Father, a mission of universal peace and reconciliation. To this end, he breathes on them and gives them the Holy Spirit. The act of breathing evokes the breath of God at the creation of man: 'Then the Lord God formed man from the dust of the ground, and breathed into his nostrils the breath of life' (Genesis 2:7; see also Wisdom 15:11; Ezekiel 37:9). The risen Jesus gives the disciples new life, granting them his own Spirit, renewing them from within and making them capable of carrying out the mission of forgiving sins.

We cannot overlook the importance of this appearance, which concludes the first day of the week, or Easter Sunday. As has already been said, we find here the fundamental elements of John's theology, in the central context of a new creation brought into being precisely through the resurrection. He stands in their midst (John 20:19), in the stance of the risen Lord. He is the Living One who can show in his own transfigured flesh the signs of his victory over death, indelible signs, impressed in his hands and his side. The author of Revelation seems to recall this very scene when he introduces 'a Lamb... standing as if it had been slain' (Revelation 5:6). In order to be understood, this paradoxical image requires a correct decoding of the interwoven symbols. The Lamb is seen standing, which means that he is victorious through the very fact of being slain. As such he is able to take the scroll from the one seated upon the throne, and to break open the seven seals (Revelation 5:7–10).

The risen Jesus gives his Spirit, making his disciples participants in the new life that springs from his wounds, from his open hands and side, the blood and water that purify, renew and pardon. Made participants in the Spirit of the risen Jesus, the disciples are sent to put the forgiveness of Jesus into practice and to communicate his peace.

EIGHT DAYS LATER: THE RISEN JESUS AND THOMAS

Here we are at the fourth scene. On the one hand it runs parallel to the previous scene (the disciples behind locked doors, the greeting of peace from the risen Jesus), and on the other hand it emerges as the summit of the entire chapter. In effect, the dialogue between Jesus and Thomas is unique in the New Testament. The appearance is set eight days later. Scripture scholars generally agree in interpreting this indication in a liturgical-ecclesial vein, an aspect that highlights the role of the Lord's Day.

The evangelist does not tell us why Thomas was absent on the evening of the first day of the week, when the risen Jesus appeared among his followers, but we do not need to speculate about it. Thomas's reaction is surprising. He rejects the testimony of the disciples ('We have seen the Lord!'), which confirms the earlier testimony of Mary Magdalene. Even more, before he will believe he demands unmistakable signs of identification of the crucified Lord (John 20:25).

Strictly speaking, Thomas 'demands nothing more than what the other disciples have already received: to put his finger, his hand into the wounds is, in fact, equivalent to seeing, to witnessing personally'.[10] But one could say that the demand of Thomas makes reference to the great scene of Golgotha, from the crucifixion until the piercing of Jesus' side.[11]

Once again, the Lord comes, in a completely sovereign and gratuitous fashion, passing through the barrier of the locked doors. As before, he stands in the midst of his disciples, and gives them peace, the biblical *shalom*, the fruit of his sacrifice. He then turns directly to Thomas. The same Jesus who had warned against the temptation of wanting to see signs in order to believe—'Unless you see signs and wonders you do not believe' (John 4:48)—now, the only time in the entire Gospel he grants such a request, satisfies Thomas's demand by inviting him to look and touch. This is a powerful invitation, with five imperatives:

'Bring (*phére*) your finger here
and look at (*íde*) my hands,
and bring (*phére*) your hand
and put (*bale*) it in my side,
and be not (*me gínou*) unbelieving, but believing!'
(John 20:27)

Jesus shows his pierced hands and open side to the doubting
disciple. They are open and generous hands that have cured and
healed, the hands into which the Father has delivered all things
(John 3:35), the strong and sure hands of the Shepherd whose
sheep no one can take away, the hands that have washed Thomas'
feet, the hands nailed to the cross.

Did Thomas actually probe the wounds? The evangelist does not
say, but he seems to suggest the contrary. There is no need to touch.
The blossoming of faith is prompted by a global and contemplative
perception that recognises the Risen One in the Pierced One: 'You
have believed because you have seen *me*' (John 20:29). Thomas
now finds himself, in a manner of speaking, in the same situation
as the beloved disciple beneath the cross: he looks at the Pierced
One and confesses his faith: 'My Lord and my God!' (John 20:28).
For him, the promise of the Master is fulfilled: 'And when I am lifted
up from the earth I will draw all men to myself' (John 12:32). In
effect, the crucified Jesus appears as the *Kýrios*, the Lord of glory
who gives life. Jesus is truly God, his God.

This second appearance of Jesus, eight days later, is like a second
Easter. It offers Thomas the possibility of establishing a vital, joyous
relationship of faith with the Lord, as had happened for the other
disciples on the evening of the first day. Even more, Thomas
becomes an example for all of us, well represented by this hard-
headed sceptic. His absence at the encounter with Jesus on the
evening of the first day puts him in a situation that, in a certain
way, is similar to our own: that of having to depend on the witness
of others. He knows that the Lord is risen because the others say

so, but he has not experienced it directly. And so arises his doubt, insidious and excruciating.[12]

The risen Jesus heals the wound of Thomas's doubt not in a private place, but in a community setting, at the meeting on the eighth day, displaying the wounds that now will identify him for ever.

'MY LORD AND MY GOD'

We have arrived at the summit, at the climax of this narrative and theological journey. At this point, we realise that the question of whether Thomas did or did not touch the wounds of his Lord is completely irrelevant. The relevance of this second appearance in comparison with the first is not found in actions but in words. Those of Jesus first, which recall Thomas's demand, and then the words that spring forth from the new Thomas. He is conquered by the crucified and risen Jesus, who displays the signs of his great mercy.

We can note that one characteristic aspect of the journey narrated in John 20 is the movement between presence and absence. We must first decode the signs of absence (the empty tomb, the burial cloths, the cloth for the head rolled up and set to one side). Then we must recognise the risen Jesus and learn a new way of experiencing the Lord. We then learn to establish a new relationship with him, no longer 'physical', but spiritual: we learn to believe in a different way.

The appearances are in fact presented as 'signs' that are not primarily meant to demonstrate the truth of Christianity or to refute its opponents, but to reveal Christ in his new mode of being after death, to sustain the faith of the disciples shaken by the events of the passion and guide them to a new relationship with the risen Jesus, passing from physical contact to the communion of faith announced beforehand in his farewell discourse (chapters 14—16).[13]

- The first step in the journey of faith in the risen Jesus can be seen in the beloved disciple, who 'saw and believed' (John 20:8). This act of faith is stimulated by the attentive observation of the burial cloths. These maintain the forms they had when the body of Jesus was present, but now they are flattened, emptied of their contents. No one has freed Jesus from the burial cloths, as was necessary for Lazarus (John 11:44). He frees himself, emerging like a butterfly from its cocoon.
- A second step in the development of faith is represented by Mary Magdalene, who recognises Jesus not because she sees him, but because she hears herself called by name: 'Mary'. The voice of Jesus, his unmistakable way of pronouncing her name, makes the weeping woman suddenly turn around and exclaim in astonishment: 'Rabboni', 'Master'.

- A third step in the journey of faith can be seen in the encounter between Jesus and the disciples on the evening of Easter. The risen Lord displays the unmistakable signs of his identity, his hands and side, and the disciples adhere to him with a faith full of joy.

- The fourth step, the summit of the entire account, is expressed by Thomas. The risen Shepherd knows his sheep. Just as he called Mary by name, so also he understands Thomas' difficulties and accepts his challenge. This is a good thing for us, because—as St Augustine noted—Thomas' doubt was more helpful to us than the immediate faith of the others.

- Jesus accepts the faith of Thomas, but he is looking beyond him, thinking of the believers of all generations, and he adds, 'Blessed are they who have not seen yet have believed!' It is not seeing Jesus physically that constitutes blessedness, but believing in him. It is spiritual contact with the Lord Jesus that constitutes the real treasure of believers.

The evangelist concludes this journey with a reference to the many things that lie outside its scope. He informs the reader that the signs collected in his account are the result of a selection among the 'many others' that Jesus performed in the presence of his disciples (John 20:30). He did not intend to write everything, but only some of the signs, which are so numerous that they do not all serve the aims of his testimony. In fact, John is writing with a very precise goal: 'so you may believe that Jesus is the Messiah, the Son of God, and so that by believing you may have life in his name' (John 20:31).

As with the signs of Jesus' historical ministry, faith is the goal of these new signs, viewed with the awareness that the risen Jesus ultimately proclaims blessed those who 'have not seen yet have believed'. This blessedness concerns us directly and resounds in the first letter of Peter, where he expresses the wonder and joy of being Christian, recognising in Jesus the crucified and risen Lord: 'Although you have not seen him you love him, and although you do not see him now you believe in him' (1 Peter 1:8).

DIALOGUING WITH THE WORD

Let us imagine ourselves with Mary Magdalene at the tomb of Jesus, at the Holy Sepulchre in Jerusalem. It's difficult to imagine a garden in that place today. Over the Lord's tomb stands the great basilica of the *Anástasis* (Resurrection), the destination of many pilgrims and visitors. Religious ceremonies are held there by ministers of many different Christian confessions—Orthodox, Catholic, Armenian, Ethiopian. Inside the little nook is a sign in Greek, which translated reads: 'The source of our royal resurrection has been manifested.' Pilgrims kneel to pray before and kiss the marble slab that covers the rock where the body of Jesus was laid. Why do so many people come, with such great devotion, to an empty tomb? We could respond with the psalmist: because all were born there! Philistia, Ethiopia, Tyre (see Psalm 87:3–7). That tomb is the mother of our rebirth.

I think of Mary Magdalene weeping: 'Why are you cast down, O my soul, and why are you disquieted within me?' (Psalm 42:11). The fundamental question returns: 'Who are you looking for?' (John 20:15). And for whom am I looking? What does the Lord's empty tomb say to me? Do I bear witness that Christian hope is not something, but *Someone*, the Living One?

The risen Jesus overcomes the disciples' resistance; he enters the room where they are gathered behind locked doors. He stands in their midst; he wants to give us his forgiveness, to heal us with his peace. What fears keep the doors of my community locked? John Paul II forcefully encouraged us throughout his pontificate: 'Do not be afraid to open the doors to Christ!' What are the fears that paralyse my mission? How do I call upon and open myself to the Spirit of the risen Jesus?

It is not in the power of the disciples to give faith to Thomas; they can only bear witness to it. But it is noteworthy that the community does not exclude Thomas; it welcomes him in spite of his doubt and continues to love him. Only Jesus can do the rest. How do I act towards those who doubt and challenge my faith? Do I allow myself to be wounded by the suffering of those who are seeking but do not find, of those who walk in darkness? And how do I live the beatitude of those who believe and love without having seen?

✝

PAUSE TO PONDER

Speak my name again, Lord Jesus.
Call to me in the way you know.
Only you know why
I am searching in the night,
the reason for my weeping.
Grant that I may recognise
the voice that calls to me.
Grant that I may turn completely
towards you who pronounce my name.
Melt my coldness with your embrace,
grant that I may worship you,
God of the new creation,
Spirit who gives life,
my Master and Saviour,
my Lord and my God.
Make me quick to proclaim to my brothers and sisters
your victory over death,
make me an ardent witness of your ascension to the Father.
Grant to me as well, Lord Jesus,
the experience of your resurrection.
Grant that I may contemplate you
with the living eyes of faith.
Grant me what you promised to Thomas,
the blessedness of those who, although they have not seen,
trust in you completely and love you.

✳

Chapter 12

THE NEW STARTING POINT IS LOVE

Our setting is the shore of the Sea of Tiberias, which according to John was the place of the third appearance of Jesus to the disciples. The surroundings are strongly evocative. The shore of that lake holds many lively memories, having been the site of the great miracle of the multiplication of the loaves and fishes.

BETWEEN CONTINUITY AND DISCONTINUITY

An attentive reading of John 21 reveals various connections with the previous chapters,[1] but also elements of tension. The evangelist has already written a solemn conclusion: 'Jesus also did many other signs in the presence of the disciples which are not written in this book, but these things have been written so you may believe that Jesus is the Messiah, the Son of God, and so that by believing you may have life in his name' (20:30–31).

Thus John declares his intention of leading his reader to faith in Jesus, Messiah and Son of God, something none of the other evangelists proclaims so openly. Surprisingly, this conclusion does not constitute the end of the Gospel. The narrative instead continues in connection with what precedes it: 'After these things Jesus showed himself to the disciples again at the Sea of Tiberias' (21:1). So should the Gospel's last chapter be characterised as an appendix or as an epilogue? In answer to this, it is interesting to observe that this chapter also presents a concluding note:

This is the disciple who bears witness to these things and has written them, and we know that his witness is true. Now there are also many other things that Jesus did; if every one of them were written down, I do not suppose the world itself would have room for the books that would be written. (21:24–25)

The second conclusion seems less emphatic than the first, and it is not as relevant from a christological perspective, containing no declaration about Jesus' divinity. It simply affirms that what was written of him is true, and, although a partial account, the evangelist's testimony is trustworthy. It also adds, with a hyperbolic expression that has parallels in ancient Jewish literature, 'I do not suppose the world itself would have room for the books that would be written.' In a certain sense, 'we will never stop writing [about Jesus], because his significance for man appears increasingly great and profound the longer we proceed through history'.[2]

In reality, chapter 21 revisits and builds upon two of the themes in chapter 20. First, it recounts the third manifestation of the risen Jesus to the disciples (21:14), inviting them to cast their nets and then to spread the proclamation of the gospel. The first two appearances in chapter 20 had been aimed at bringing the disciples to believe in Jesus as Lord and God (vv. 28, 31). Moreover, chapter 21 elaborates on the relationship between Peter and the beloved disciple (vv. 7–8 and 15–23), sketched out earlier in the account of the two men running to the tomb (20:3–8).

With both these specific elements and the overall perspective in mind, it seems that John 21 deserves to be considered more than an appendix. It is a true epilogue, corresponding in a way to the prologue. John 1:1–18 forms its own separate unity, describing the 'before'—the eternal origin of the incarnate *Logos* and the general meaning of his coming. In a similar way, chapter 21 depicts the 'after'—what follows Jesus' death and resurrection, or his presence in the Church's mission. 'After presenting Jesus' conferral of the mission to his disciples (20:21–23; cf. Acts 1:8), the evangelist presents a paradigmatic episode of this mission, for the purpose of indicating what the conditions are for bearing fruit, and the role that Jesus has in this.'[3]

The passage is divided into two sections. The first (vv. 1–14) includes the episode set at the Sea of Tiberias, while the second (vv. 15–23) contains the dialogue between Jesus and Simon Peter, and the comparison with the beloved disciple.

BUT THAT NIGHT THEY CAUGHT NOTHING

Our setting is the Sea of Tiberias, where an appearance will take place that is not intended for all of the disciples, but only for seven of them, a number symbolic of completeness. The first to enter the scene is Peter, who proposes to go fishing. He is followed, in order, by:

- Thomas, called Didymus ('twin')
- Nathanael from Cana
- Zebedee's two sons (James and John)
- Two other disciples who are not named

It seems like a return to their former way of life,[4] when they were simply concerned about fishing for fish, and not persons: 'Simon Peter said to them, "I am going out to fish." They said to him, "We will go with you, too." They went out and got in the boat and that night they caught nothing' (John 21:3).

'Go out' and 'get in' are verbs of the exodus. The Hebrews go out from Egypt and go up toward Jerusalem, in the promised land. But what do these verbs mean in relation to the new situation? In the initiative of Peter and his companions, we can perhaps glimpse the faint outline of a ministerial decision. Jesus had told them, 'I will make you fishers of men!' (Matthew 4:19; Mark 1:17). And if we read the passage literally, we can conclude: 'They went out...

and got in... they caught nothing.' It is not enough to decide to go out, to get into the boat and to challenge the sea. Our missionary decision is not enough.

Another passage from the Gospel of Luke comes to mind (5: 1–10). It was at the beginning of Jesus' ministry in Galilee.[5] After speaking to and instructing the crowd seated on the bank of the lake, the Master gets into Simon's boat and asks him to go out into the deep and cast his nets. Simon objects that they have laboured the entire night without catching anything, but he adds, 'At your word I will lower the nets.' And he is not disappointed. On the contrary, he has to call for another boat because they catch so many fish. Simon is so astonished that he throws himself at the knees of Jesus, saying, 'Leave me, Lord, for I am a sinful man!' But Jesus does not withdraw; instead, he calls Simon even closer to himself: 'Do not be afraid; from now on you will be catching men' (Luke 5:10). An analogous situation is presented in John 21: that night the fishermen had caught nothing. Without Jesus, the Church could work the entire night but it would toil in vain, with nothing to show for it!

WHEN IT WAS ALREADY DAWN

At dawn, Jesus appears at the lake shore. First, we note the indication of time. It is early morning, when one still can't see quite clearly. Mary Magdalene had also gone to the tomb early in the morning, when it was still dark (see John 20:1). Jesus appears when the darkness collides with the advancing light. He is on the lake shore, but the disciples do not recognise that it is he, as had happened at the tomb for Mary Magdalene.

Once again, Jesus takes the initiative in the conversation:

Jesus said to them, 'Children, do you have any fish?' They answered him, 'No.' Then he said to them, 'Cast the net to the right side of the boat and you will find some.' So they cast it, and now they were unable to draw it in because of the number of fish. (John 21:5–6)

The disciples' abrupt response to Jesus' question shows their great discouragement: 'No.' What a disappointment to return from fishing without a single fish! Jesus overcomes this moment of bitterness and disillusionment: 'Cast the net... and you will find...'

But why does he specify 'over to the right side'? The right-hand side is a recurring element in the Bible and has various meanings, which are not always charged with theological symbolism. The name Benjamin, for example, means 'son of the right hand', or 'of blessing'. The right-hand side indicates the place of honour; it is given to prominent and respected persons. Jesus sits 'at the right hand of the Father', meaning that he has the place of honour, the glory of the Son. The elect will also be placed at the right hand of the king, according to Matthew 25: the shepherd 'will set the sheep at his right' (v. 33). Casting the net over the right side could thus allude to the possibility of salvation that is opened for the pagan peoples as well. As we will see, these people are indicated by the symbolic number of 153 fish.

The most important point is the necessity to trust in the word of Jesus: 'Cast the net...' Despite the fact that the night, the ideal time for fishing, has passed without anything to show for it, the dawn holds wonderful surprises when one trusts in Jesus: the result is staggering, an enormous catch. The disciples even fear that the net could break because of all the fish. Yet it does not break. The net of Peter, like the garment of Jesus, is the symbol of the Church's unity.

'IT IS THE LORD!'

And so it happens that the sign leads to the recognition of the risen
Jesus. As before at the tomb, here as well the intuitive vision of the
beloved disciple arrives first:

So the disciple Jesus loved said to Peter, 'It is the Lord!' Simon
Peter, when he heard that it was the Lord, put on his outer
garment—he was stripped—and threw himself into the sea. Then
the other disciples came with the boat—they were not far from
land, about a hundred yards away—dragging the net of fish.
(John 21:7–8)

The one who intuits first is the beloved disciple, but the one who
jumps into the sea immediately is Simon Peter. Wonderful! The
evangelist seems to call attention deliberately to a detail that is
incongruent at first sight. Why does Peter put on his garment before
jumping into the water to go and meet the Lord? According to some
interpreters, Peter was wearing a small undergarment, suited for the
work of fishing, and before he jumped into the water he would have
secured it with a cincture in order to swim more easily. But his outer
garment would have done nothing but obstruct his movements.
However one interprets this detail, there seems to be a dynamic
at play between being naked and being clothed, reinforced by the
expression 'put on his outer garment', previously used in reference
to Jesus in the context of the washing of the feet (John 13:4–5).
    One could say that Peter is 'stripped' because he has not
assumed the attitude of Jesus, his service to the point of death.
For this reason, his mission (fishing) has not borne any fruit. 'Now,
finally, he understands. He secures that garment like Jesus had put
on the towel in order to serve. To express his willingness to give his
life, he throws himself into the water. He demonstrates that he is
willing to serve to the point of death. Now he understands what
Jesus had done for him by washing his feet.'[6] Peter feels the need

to fasten his garment, to prepare himself to meet the Lord. And in this perspective, he exhorts Christians to 'gird up the loins of your mind', fixing their hope upon the grace that comes to them in the revelation of Jesus Christ (see 1 Peter 1:13).

Peter arrives first, while the other disciples follow him, dragging on the ground the net full of fish. It is important to bring the boat ashore. Everyone has his role in the community. But all share in the fire that gives light and warmth and in the fragrant meal, the good bread and fish prepared by Jesus.

'COME, HAVE BREAKFAST'

On the shore of the lake is a charcoal fire. The detail is interesting. It is not a great bonfire that could have been seen from the boat on the lake, but a charcoal fire, which they see only when they reach land: 'So as they were coming up onto land they saw a charcoal fire started and a fish laid on it and bread' (John 21:9). Those glowing coals are magnificent for cooking fish, but to me they also recall the vocation and mission of Isaiah, when the seraph touches the prophet's lips with the burning coal, freeing him from the impurity of sin and thus qualifying him to proclaim the word of the Lord (Isaiah 6:6–8). In John 21 as well we are in a context of mission; the Church is called to set out into the deep and cast its nets, and no less to be purified and nourished by Christ.

Bread and fish: an excellent breakfast for someone who has worked all night! But evidently that bread and those fish allude to something else, to the great sign performed by Jesus on the shore of that lake in the context of the feast of Passover, the miracle that had prompted the exclamation: 'Truly this is the Prophet who is to come into the world!' (John 6:14). Once again, Jesus takes the initiative:

Jesus said to them, 'Bring some of the fish you caught just now.'
So Simon Peter went aboard and dragged the net to land, full of
large fish—one hundred and fifty-three—yet, even though there
were so many, the net was not split. Jesus said to them, 'Come,
eat breakfast.' None of the disciples dared to ask him, 'Who are
you?' because they knew it was the Lord. Jesus came and took the
bread and gave it to them, and likewise the fish. (John 21:10–13)

On top of the charcoal fire is the fish, which for the first Christians
was the symbol of Jesus himself. In fact, the letters that spell the
word in Greek, *ichthus*, 'fish', also correspond to the initials of the
phrase: 'Jesus Christ, Son of God, Saviour'. The meal is ready; the
fish cooks on the fire. The disciples see the same foods that the
Lord had distributed to the crowd: bread and fish (see John 6:
9–11). The Eucharist is the great sign of the welcome of Jesus.

But the Lord's gift does not exclude our collaboration. On the
contrary, he asks for this: 'Bring some of the fish you caught just
now' (John 21:10). The fish Jesus has prepared is ready, but he also
wants this one meal to include the fish that you have caught! He
wants to add to his gift the fruit of our labour:

*The community lives by Jesus and by his love, but also by mission, love
of neighbour, which realises and expresses love for Jesus (John 14:21);
this love is also his gift (the Spirit), but it demands active collaboration on everyone's part. These two are inseparable, and both give life to
the community. This single but twofold love is also expressed in two forms:
in the effort of work and in the joy of the meal with Jesus.*[7]

The detail of the 153 large fish is intriguing. This was thought
to be the number of species of fish, a symbol of all the races or
peoples of the world. And they all fit into the net, which 'was not
torn'. For John, this verb is very important. He uses it in regard to
Jesus' tunic, woven in a single piece from top to bottom, that the
soldiers decided not to tear. The net that does not tear symbolises

the Church. Although it gathers within itself all races of people in extraordinary numbers, it is destined to remain one.

LOVE: THE CONDITION FOR FEEDING
THE LORD'S FLOCK

After breakfast, Jesus asks Peter, 'Simon son of John, do you love me more than they do?' It is interesting to observe the lexical variation present in this dialogue between Jesus and Peter.[8] As noted, the Greek language has three fundamental terms to speak of love:

- *Éros* indicates erotic desire, the attraction of physical beauty.
- *Philía* accentuates the sentiment of friendship, of benevolence.
- *Agápe*, above all in the context of the New Testament, designates the supreme love of charity. John says that God is *agápe* (1 John 4:8).

Jesus, then, interrogates Peter on supreme love: 'Do you love me?' (*agapás me*)? If Jesus had asked this question before the passion, for example in the context of the Last Supper, I think that Peter would not have hesitated to respond to him with the same verb (see John 13:37, where the apostle says he is ready to give his life for the Master). But now, the devastating experience of his betrayal stops him (see Luke 22:61–62, where Jesus looks at Peter and Peter weeps). Jesus has truly loved to the point of giving his life, but not Peter! For this reason, he dare not respond to the Master with the verb *agapáo*. The experience of sin has made him humble and aware of the distance between himself and his Lord. He responds with the verb *philéo*, employing all of the sincerity of his friendship: 'Yes, Lord, you know that I love you!' (John 21:15).

The Lord insists, and for a second time he asks Peter for the love of *agápe*: 'Simon son of John, do you love me?' He replies, 'Yes, Lord, you know that I love you!' Jesus says, 'Tend my sheep!' (v.

16). Peter again replies with *philéo*, the verb of friendship, all that he can honestly vouch for in the bitter awareness of having disowned Jesus.

The third time, we see the same verb in both the question and the answer. The one who cedes, however, is not Peter, but the Master. Jesus replaces the verb *agapáo* with *philéo* as if bringing himself down to Peter's level:

He said to him a third time, 'Simon son of John, do you love me?' Peter was distressed because he said to him a third time, 'Do you love me?' and he said to him, 'Lord, you know everything; you know that I love you!' He said to him, 'Feed my sheep!' (v. 17)

This variation suggests that Jesus accepts Peter's love. Humble and sincere love is the only condition required for nourishing the flock. It is as if to say that we must take care of others and 'feed the Lord's flock' not with the love we would like to have, but with all the love we in fact do have. Yet we must not stop there. The risen Jesus proclaims to his apostle the supreme goal of love, the gift of life:

'Amen, amen, I say to you, when you were young you fastened your belt and went where you wanted, but when you are old you will stretch out your hands and another will fasten you and bring you where you do not wish to go.' He said this to indicate by what type of death he would glorify God. After saying this he said to him, 'Follow me!' (vv. 18–19)

On closer inspection, John 21:15–19 presents three elements linked in a sequence that is valuable for the spiritual and ministerial dynamic:

1. Question and answer about love
2. The task of feeding the Lord's flock
3. The invitation to follow Jesus

The pastoral mandate is in the central position between love and the following of Jesus. We cannot wait for our love to become perfect before taking care of others. Rather, beginning humbly with the love that we have, we are called to follow Jesus beyond *philía* to the perfection of *agápe*. In conclusion, the risen Lord rehabilitates Peter on the basis of love, the sole condition for the ministry of pastoral care. And it is not prideful love, but humble love that permits us to follow in the footsteps of the one great Shepherd.

But Peter is not alone in following the footsteps of the great Shepherd: 'When Peter turned he saw the disciple Jesus loved following' and the Master says of him, 'If I want him to stay till I come, what is it to you? Follow me!' (vv. 20, 22). He is the disciple 'who bears witness to these things and has written them, and we know that his witness is true' (v. 24). These words reflect the tradition that the evangelist lived a long life, but also, and in particular, the enduring testimony of his Gospel throughout the generations. Peter and John, pastoral authority and anointed testimony: two realities destined to endure. They mark the passage from the direct ministry of Jesus to that of the disciples, the beginning and model of the Church's mission in the world.

DIALOGUING WITH THE WORD

Let's imagine ourselves on the shore of the Sea of Tiberias, so rich with the memory of Gospel events. Let's enter into the scene of the third appearance of the risen Jesus. Let's ask for the gift of experiencing his presence in the life and mission of the Church.

 The new day begins with the presence of Jesus, who makes the mission of his friends, his community, bear fruit. We, too, sometimes labour in vain, working through the entire night without catching anything. What obstructs my ministry, my apostolic service? Am I aware of the mission I have received and the grace that comes to me from the Lord, or do I act as though I were on my own and everything depended on me? How and where do I discover the presence of the Lord?

What does it mean to 'cast the nets' at the command of the risen Jesus? What do these words mean for me, in the concrete situations of my life? How do I overcome moments of failure and disappointment?

How much attention do I reserve for the gift and service of each person? Not all have the intuitive vision of John, but it is important that all work together to bring to shore the boat full of fish that the Lord gives to the community. How do I see the role of Peter, of John and of the other disciples?

I dwell upon the image of the fire that the disciples see as soon as they reach land. They couldn't see it when they were in the boat, concentrating on fishing. Those glowing coals warm their hearts and purify their lips. On the night of his betrayal, Peter tried to warm himself beside the fire kindled by the soldiers and guards, but his lips uttered lies and denial (John 18:18). Now the fire kindled by Jesus revives the joy of togetherness. What experience do I have of the Lord, of his fire?

Jesus also invites us: 'Come, eat.' For me, too, Jesus kindles a charcoal fire. For me, too, he gives his eucharistic bread. The Lord waits for me and appreciates my work, my effort. Do I allow myself to be welcomed and nourished at his table? How do I respond to Jesus' question of love? Can I say with the sincerity of Peter, 'You know that I love you?' Am I able to appreciate the gifts of the others who follow the Lord as I do?

✝

PAUSE TO PONDER

Lord Jesus, you wait for us always
on the shore of life.
You know well that we can work
and labour in vain,
while you have called us
in order that we may bear fruit,
and that our fruit may endure.
Grant us to trust in you.
Grant us to throw out the nets
once again at your word.
Wash us in the sea of your mercy,
warm us with the fire of your Spirit,
and nourish us with your bread and your fish,
with your holy Eucharist.
Thank you for not wanting to do everything yourself,
for desiring to unite the fruit of our labour
with your gift.
You honour our missionary dignity
and assure us of your presence.
You ask only for love.
Grant us, then, to begin again
from the starting point of humble love.
Grant us to follow in your footsteps,
O good Shepherd,
that we may take loving care
of every person you entrust to us,
and of all humanity.

✳

NOTES

Introduction

1   *Ignatius to the Magnesians*, VIII, 2: trans. K. Lake, *Apostolic Fathers* (Cambridge, MA: Harvard University Press, 1977), Vol. I, 205.

2   'The retrospective outlook is, for John, both a theological framework and a narrative perspective', cited by Klaus Wengst, *Il Vangelo di Giovanni*, I (Brescia, Italy: Queriniana, 2005), 121.

3   Alain Marchadour, *I Personaggi del Vangelo di Giovanni: Specchio per una cristologia narrativa* (Bologna, Italy: EDB, 2007), 11.

Chapter 1

1   'As expressed by Andrew, the concept of the Messiah must be interpreted in view of two factors: (a) the phrase that he heard from John the Baptist ('the Lamb of God'; 1:36), and (b) the translation offered by the evangelist ('the Anointed One'; 1:41).' See J. Mateos and J. Barreto, *Il Vangelo di Giovanni: Analisi linguistica e commento esegetico* (Assisi, Italy: Cittadella, 2000), 113.

Chapter 2

1   Mateos and Barreto, *Il Vangelo di Giovanni*, 125.

2   For this proposed interpretation, see Y. Simoens, *Secondo Giovanni. Una traduzione e un'interpretazione* (Bologna, Italy: EDB, 2000), 113.

3   Today he would probably be classified as a 'skilled labourer': compare G. Magnani, *Origini del cristianesimo*, Vol 2. *Gesù costruttore e maestro, l'ambiente: nuove prospettive* (Assisi, Italy: Cittadella, 1996).

4   Mateos and Barreto, *Il Vangelo di Giovanni*, 122.

5   Benedict XVI, *God Is Love* (Boston: Pauline Books & Media, 2005), no. 7.

6   Song of Songs 8:5; for further study see E. Bosetti, *Cantico dei cantici: 'Tu che il mio cuore ama', Estasi e ricerca* (Milan, Italy: Edizioni San Paolo, Cinisello Balsamo, 2001).

Chapter 3

1   F.J. Moloney, *Mary: Woman and Mother* (Homebush, New South Wales, Australia: St Paul Publications, 1988), 33.
2   Emphasis in scripture.
3   A. Niccacci and O. Battaglia, *Il Vangelo dello spirito, Vol. 5: Secondo Giovanni* (Assisi, Italy: Edizioni Porziuncola, 1979), 28.
4   A. Serra, *Nato da Donna... ricerche bibliche su Maria di Nazaret* (Rome: Marianum, 1992), 172.

Chapter 4

1   He does not go to Jesus in the daytime 'because it is not necessary that others know that he keeps contacts that might discredit him in public opinion' (Wengst, *Il Vangelo di Giovanni*, 128).
2   We find again the term *basiléia* associated to the first person pronoun in John 18:36, in Jesus' reply to Pilate: 'My kingdom is not of this world; if my kingdom were of this world my attendants would fight so that I wouldn't be handed over.'
3   Rudolf Schnackenburg, *Il Vangelo di Giovanni: Testo greco e traduzione. Parte prima: Introduzione e commento ai capp. 1–4* (Brescia, Italy: Paideia, 1973), 529.
4   Joseph Ratzinger (Pope Benedict XVI), *Jesus of Nazareth* (New York: Doubleday, 2007), 240.
5   Wengst, *Il Vangelo di Giovanni*, 718.

Chapter 5

1   Augustine, *Treatises on John*, 15:10–12.

Chapter 6

1   The synoptic Gospels contain Jesus' saying about the narrow gate: 'How narrow the gate and difficult the way leading to life, and few are those who find it!' (Matthew 7:14; see also Luke 13:23–24). The fourth evangelist refers this saying directly to Jesus, and colours the various symbolic details with christological meaning. Jesus is the gate, the way to life: 'I am the gate. Whoever comes in through me will be saved' (John 10:9).
2   In the letter to the Hebrews, the figure of the 'pioneer of their salvation' (2:10; see 12:2) is taken up again at the conclusion with the image of 'the great shepherd of the sheep' (13:20). On this topic, see E. Bosetti,

'*Il Pastore, quello grande: Risonanze e funzione conclusiva di Eb 13:20–21*' in J.E. Aguilar Chiu, F. Manzi, F. Urso, C. Zesati Estrada (eds.), '*Il Verbo di Dio è vivo.*' *Studi sul Nuovo Testamento in onore del Cardinale Albert Vanhoye, SJ* (Rome: Pontifical Biblical Institute, 2007), 443–461.

3 These terms are used in reference to Judas Iscariot (John 12:6) and Barabbas (18:40).

4 The meaning of the phrase is polemical: those who came before Jesus claiming messianic authority were in fact shown to be thieves and robbers. Their purpose was death. These words can be seen as an attack on the movement of the Zealots and on their idea of messianic liberation. For Jesus, the messianism of Barabbas is larceny.

   In AD70, the temple was destroyed and Jerusalem was reduced to a pile of rubble. Against this background, the words of Jesus sound like a bitter reflection: those who came in a messianic disguise and filled your heads with nationalism were all thieves and robbers, they've taken everything from you, even the temple! During the Jewish war, the first Christians imitated the behaviour of their Master and did not align themselves with the Zealots against the Romans, but instead fled to Pella in Jordan.

5 See 13:37–38; 15:13; 1 John 3:16. In the fourth Gospel, the preposition *hyper* (for) is almost always found in a sacrificial context: Jesus gives his flesh *for* the life of the world (6:51); he gives his life *for* his sheep (10:11, 15); he dies *for* the people, in order to (*hyper*) unite the scattered children of God (11:50–52; see 18:14); he sanctifies himself *for* the disciples (17:19). In particular, there is a strong connection with the discourse on the bread of life: 'the bread that I will give *for* (*hyper*) the life of the world is my flesh' (6:51).

6 See Schnackenburg, *Il Vangelo di Giovanni*, II, 498–501.

7 'To Jesus, Good Shepherd' in *Le preghiere della Famiglia Paolina* (San Paolo, Brazil: Alba, 1985), 118–119.

Chapter 7

1 Her profile is sketched by Luke (10:38–42) and John (11:1—12:11), who agree in presenting her as a practical, straightforward and generous woman, linked to Jesus by a deep friendship. Luke introduces her first, as the owner of the house (10:38). But not John, who qualifies both Martha and Lazarus in relation to Mary (11:1–2).

2 The phrase 'live for ever (eternal life)' appears in the Bible for the first time here (Daniel 12:2). It is contrasted with a situation of 'everlasting disgrace', meaning an irreversible defeat, definitive failure: see Psalm 78:66.

3   When the apostle Paul is brought on trial before the Sanhedrin, he will use this situation to defend himself: 'Now Paul realised that one part of the assembly was made up of Sadducees while the other part was made up of Pharisees, so he cried out, "My brothers, I am a Pharisee, the son of Pharisees! I am on trial for hoping in the resurrection of the dead!" When he said this a dispute arose between the Pharisees and Sadducees, and the assembly was divided. For the Sadducees say that there's no resurrection, no angels, and no spirits, while the Pharisees believe in all of them. So there was a tremendous clamour' (Acts 23:6–9).

4   This episode is also narrated in Matthew 22:23–32 and Luke 20:27–38.

5   In a novel by J. Saramago (*The Gospel According to Jesus Christ*, Lisbon, Portugal: 1991), Martha asks Jesus not to revive her brother, because no one has ever committed so many sins in life as to deserve to die twice!

6   The account of the anointing of Jesus by a woman is known to all four evangelists, but each one tells the story in a different way, at least in some of the details. So doubt arises about whether we are dealing with the same story or not. According to Morna D. Hooker, we have here 'an interesting example of the way in which a story could be adapted and given different interpretations by different evangelists' (*The Gospel According to Saint Mark* [Peabody, MA: Hendrickson, 1991], 327). In particular, John's account presents points of similarity with the story in Luke 7:36–50, but, unlike the anonymous sinner, Mary of Bethany does not shed tears on the feet of Jesus, but only anoints them with perfumed oil, the purest nard.

Chapter 8

1   'Defending the rank of another means defending one's own; not accepting the gesture of Jesus means not being willing to act as he does… Jesus' initiative creates a group of equals; the leader abandons his post to make himself equal to his followers; this disorients [Peter], and he refuses. Like the multitude of Jerusalem, he wants Jesus to be leader (12; 13, "king of Israel"); he does not accept his service, nor, moreover, that he should die for him (12:34; 13:37).' Mateos and Barreto, *Il Vangelo di Giovanni*, 557–558.

2   T. Bello, *Omelie e scritti quaresimali* (Molfetta, Italy: Editoria Luce e Vita, 1994), 140.

3   See G. Salonia, *Odòs. La Via della vita* (Bologna, Italy: EDB, 2007).

4   This theme is especially dear to John, who introduces it from the very first scene of his Gospel with the allusion to Jacob's ladder; see John 1:51.

5   These two terms are already found paired in Exodus 34:6, in which it

is said that Yahweh passed before Moses crying, 'The Lord, the Lord, a merciful and gracious God, slow to anger and rich in kindness and fidelity (chèsed we-emèt).'

6   J. Alberione, *To the Pastorelle Sisters*, 1959.

7   St Thomas Aquinas, *Commento al Vangelo di San Giovanni*, Vol. III (Rome: Città Nuova, 1992), 173.

8   This theme is of great importance for the fourth evangelist, who emphasises that Jesus also deliberately chose Judas, the traitorous disciple (see John 13:18). He anticipates this in the synagogue of Capernaum, at the conclusion of the discourse on the bread of life, a discourse that is terribly disconcerting for his audience when Jesus specifies that the bread is his 'flesh'. 'Because of this', the evangelist notes, 'many of his disciples turned back and no longer walked with him' (John 6:66). But Jesus 'knew from the beginning who they were who didn't believe, and who it was who would hand him over' (v. 64). His question, 'Did I not choose you Twelve?' (v. 70), manifests the sovereignty of his initiative, but does not remove the responsibility of the reply that is played out every day in the freedom and concreteness of history.

9   To the man freed from a legion of demons who asks to be allowed to follow him, Jesus entrusts this mission: 'Go off to your home, to your own people, and proclaim to them everything the Lord has done for you and how he had mercy on you' (Mark 5:19). See also the remarks on following Jesus in Luke 9:57–62.

10 On the connection between the image of the woman in labour and the woman-mother beside the cross, see John Paul II's *Mulieris Dignitatem*, no. 19.

11 John Paul II, Apostolic Letter *Mulieris Dignitatem* (Rome: Libreria Editrice Vaticana, 1988), no. 19.

12 See U. Vanni, *L'Apocalisse* (Bologna, Italy: EDB, 1988), 345ff.

13 Prayer '*Absorbeat*' in *Fonti Francescane: Nuova edizione*, edited by E. Caroli (Padua, Italy: Editrici Francescane, 2004), 191.

Chapter 9

1   This designation appears incorrect to S. Grasso, *Il Vangelo di Giovanni: Commento esegetico e teologico* (Rome: Città Nuova, 2008), 657–684. A contrary view is held by Simoens, *Secondo Giovanni*, 639–664.

2   There are many echoes of the Lord's Prayer in the prayer of John 17; Simoens (*Secondo Giovanni*, 649–659) has collected them into six points without minimising the Johannine accents.

3   This is according to Rudolf Bultmann, as quoted by K. Wengst, who observes: 'In the Gospel of John, Jesus spoke of God above all as his Father. Thus it is here that God is made known as the Father of Jesus Christ. He is, however, the same God whose name Moses asked to know (Exodus 3:13), who presented himself as the God of Abraham, the God of Isaac and the God of Jacob (Exodus 3:6), and who promised his presence to those who would journey with him (Exodus 3:14). The Gospel [of John] made it possible that, through Jesus Christ, men and women who come from various nations might find access to the God of Israel by learning to know him as the Father of Jesus Christ. They believe that God in Jesus, precisely in the Crucifixion, pronounced his "Behold I come" and they believe that he *glorified* him' (*Il Vangelo di Giovanni*, 621).

4   Mateos and Berreto, *Il Vangelo di Giovanni*, 672.

5   Mateos and Berreto, *Il Vangelo di Giovanni*, 672.

6   Niccacci and Battaglia, *Il Vangelo secondo Giovanni*, 191.

7   'Congregation for the Doctrine of the Faith, Letter to the Bishops of the Catholic Church on Some Aspects of the Church Understood as Communion *Communionis Notio*' (May 28, 1992), 4: AAS 85 (1993), 840.

8   C. Lubich, *L'unità e Gesù abbandonato* (Rome: Città Nuova, 1984), 26–27.

Chapter 10

1   See Wengst, *Il Vangelo di Giovanni*, 637ff.

2   See Matthew 26:36; Mark 14:32. The name 'Gethsemane' is related to the presence of an olive press.

3   The Greek verb *paradídomi* embraces two meanings that should not be opposed to each other, in part because we find them within the same context: handing over and betraying.

4   Wengst, *Il Vangelo di Giovanni*, p. 645.

5   John freely takes a well-known fact in Christian tradition (see Mark 14:47) and enriches it with details interwoven with various symbolic elements. First, the name 'Malchus' means 'king'. Also, the right ear was the part of the body that was smeared with blood from the sacrifice when the high priest received his consecration. To cut off the right ear of Malchus therefore symbolises depriving him of priesthood and royalty. In any case, the interpretation Jesus offered is fundamental: he intends to 'drink the cup the Father has given me' without resisting or violence.

6   Pilate was governor of the province of Judea from AD26 to 36. Philo writes of him: 'It was not so much to honour Tiberius as to insult the people that he dedicated some golden shields in Herod's residence in the Holy City'

(*Legatio ad Gaium*, 299). [Trans. note: from Italian translation, not from original.] His tendency towards provocation is also attested by the coins minted under his rule, which reproduced symbols of emperor worship (see Wengst, *Il Vangelo di Giovanni*, 665).

7   C.M. Martini, *Il Vangelo secondo Giovanni nell'esperienza degli esercizi spirituali* (Rome: Borla), 140–149.

8   'Barabbas' is a surname meaning literally 'son of his father'. A variant of Matthew recalls that the first name of Barabbas was Jesus, the same as the Nazarene, but with different prospects of salvation: see E. Bosetti, *Matthew: The Journey Toward Hope* (Boston: Pauline Books & Media, 2006), p. 51.

9   The scene of flagellation and mockery is recounted more extensively in Mark 15:15–19 and Matthew 27:26–30. The Roman *flagellum* was made of leather, fitted with bits of bone and metal, and was believed to be the cruellest instrument available for whipping, tearing the flesh from the bone in bloody shreds, so much so that flagellation alone could lead to death. The torturers were generally slaves who were given this job, while the condemned person was bound to a column.

10   T.L. Brodie, *The Gospel According to John* (New York: Oxford University Press, 1993), 545.

11   See Matthew 27:39–44; Mark 15:29–32; Luke 23:35.

12   The division of the mantle of the prophet Ahijah foreshadows the division of the kingdom after the death of Solomon (1 Kings 11:30–31). Moreover, in regard to the seamless tunic, Flavius Josephus writes, 'This tunic (of the high priest) is not divided into two pieces with seams at the shoulders and sides, but is woven into a single piece (with an opening at the neck not cut across' (*Ant.* 3, 161). [Trans. note: from Italian translation, not from original] Wengst comments: 'The similarity between this description and that of John 19:23b induces one to think that this verse could also allude to a high priestly function for the dying Jesus: he accomplishes reconciliation in the sense meant in 11:50–52 and 18:14' (*Il Vangelo di Giovanni*, 703).

Chapter 11

1   All four Gospels attest that Jesus rose the first day after the Sabbath, or the first day of the week: see Mark 16:2, 9; Matthew 28:1; Luke 24:1; John 20:1. But more than the others, Luke and John emphasise the liturgical and ecclesial implications of this event, and they colour in eucharistic tones the meals with the risen Jesus: see Luke 24:13–35 and John 21:4–14. According to Acts 20:7, the community of Jesus' disciples gathered on the first day of the week for the breaking of the bread, the celebration of

the Eucharist.

2   The deepening of this theological perspective prompted St Ignatius of Antioch to say that we no longer live 'for the Sabbath, but for the Lord's Day, in which life blossomed for us thanks to him and his death' (*To the Magnesians*, 9, 1) [Trans. note: from Italian translation, not from original]

3   The Acts of the Apostles presents Peter and John as companions in prayer, but also in suffering for their witness to the name of Jesus. They go up together to the temple to pray, and after Peter obtains a miracle at the 'Beautiful Gate' of the temple, they are both imprisoned (Acts 3:1—4:3). But at the end they are happy to have suffered for the sake of the name of Jesus (5:41). The pairing of Peter and Paul may be more familiar to us, but the one that associates Peter and John is no less rich in inspiration, with the multiple suggestions and resonance that derive from this, like the interweaving of authority and anointing, prophecy and ministry.

4   He will also be the one who first recognises the Lord on the shore of the Sea of Tiberias: see John 21:7.

5   'There is no other way to call a woman that has the same warmth,' notes B. Rigaux, *Dio l'ha risuscitato: Esegesi e teologia biblica*. Preface by Albert Descamps (Rome: Edizioni Paoline, 1976), 323–324.

6   This aspect was grasped well by Rabanus Maurus, *De vita beatae Mariae Magdalenae*, 27 (PL 112, 1474): '*Salvator… ascensionis suae eam ad apostolos instituit apostolam*' ('The Saviour… made her [Mary Magdalene] the apostle to the apostles of his ascension').

7   For a deeper exploration, see E. Bosetti, '*Il Figlio e i figli di Dio: Etica filiale del Nuovo Testamento*', RTM XXXVI (2004), no. 142, 227–245.

8   '*Facta est Apostolorum Apostola*' (Thomas Aquinas, *In Johannem Evangelistam Expositio*, c. XX, L. III, 6).

9   A. Comastri and F. Cacucci, '*Presentazione*', in *Senza la domenica non possiamo vivere: Linee teologico-pastorali del XXIV Congresso Eucaristico Nazionale* (Bologna: EDB, 2004), 7.

10   Niccacci and Battaglia, *Il Vangelo secondo Giovanni*, 218.

11   See U. Vanni, '*Il crocifisso risorto di Tommaso* (John 20:24–29). *Un'ipotesi di lavoro*', *Studia Patavina*, 50, no. 3 (2003), 753–775.

12   Luke shows that all the disciples are to some extent in the same condition as Thomas: they are unable to believe in the resurrection; they think they are seeing a ghost. In order to persuade them, Jesus says, without referring explicitly to the marks of the crucifixion: 'Look at my hands and my feet, that it is I myself. Touch me and see' (Luke 24:39).

13   Niccacci and Battaglia, *Il Vangelo secondo Giovanni*, 213.

Chapter 12

1 A clear connection is perceived here with John 6, but also with the scenes set in the upper room and the account of the passion; the triple denial of Peter corresponds symmetrically with the triple request for love by Jesus. Even the charcoal fire on the shore recalls the fire on the night of Peter's denial.

2 G. Segalla, *Evangelo e Vangeli* (Bologna: EDB, 1993), p. 316.

3 Mateos and Barreto, *Il Vangelo di Giovanni*, 835.

4 We also find this return in the synoptic Gospels (Matthew 28:7, 10, 16–17; Mark 14:28; 16:7). In reality, here the vocational transition is realised from ordinary fisherman to fishers of men.

5 See E. Bosetti, *Luke: The Song of God's Mercy* (Boston: Pauline Books & Media, 2006), pp. 70–75.

6 Mateos and Barreto, *Il Vangelo di Giovanni*, 845–6.

7 Mateos and Barreto, *Il Vangelo di Giovanni*, 847.

8 Benedict XVI dedicated his first encyclical, *Deus Caritas Est*, to the theme of love. In it, we find a direct discussion of *éros* and *agápe*, but almost nothing of *philía*, which in this case is decisive for understanding Peter's experience, in accord with what Jesus himself had said to his disciples in the upper room: 'I have called you friends (*phíloi*)' (John 15:15). In the dialogue between Jesus and Simon Peter, nonetheless, there appears the truth of what the pope asserts at the conclusion of the first part of his encyclical: 'Love of God and love of neighbour are thus inseparable, they form a single commandment... Love grows through love. Love is "divine" because it comes from God and unites us to God; through this unifying process it makes us a "we" which transcends our divisions and makes us one, until in the end God is "all in all"' (no. 18).

THE APOSTLES' CREED

A USER'S GUIDE

Marshall D. Johnson

'I believe in God, the Father almighty, creator of heaven and earth...' In the majestic opening phrases of the Apostles' Creed we hear the passion of the early Church to define and substantiate the core of Christian belief. In the face of numerous prevailing heresies, the Apostles' Creed declared the uniqueness of the Three-in-One God and the universal scope of the divine work of salvation.

This book is an accessible introduction to what remains the most widely used of all Christendom's confessions of faith. Going through each phrase of the Apostles' Creed in turn, the author unpacks the meaning and explains its significance both historically and for Christians today. While the creed does not spell out how we are to live as disciples day by day, it is a unique 'rule of faith' that provides continuity of belief from generations past into our own time.

Includes material for group discussion.

ISBN 978 1 84101 679 5   £5.99
Available from your local Christian bookshop or, in case of difficulty, direct from BRF using the order form opposite.
You may also visit www.brfonline.org.uk

ORDERFORM

REF	TITLE		PRICE	QTY	TOTAL
679 5	The Apostles' Creed		£5.99		

POSTAGE AND PACKING CHARGES					Postage and packing	
Order value	UK	Europe	Surface	Air Mail	Donation	
£7.00 & under	£1.25	£3.00	£3.50	£5.50	TOTAL	
£7.10–£30.00	£2.25	£5.50	£6.50	£10.00		
Over £30.00	FREE	prices on request				

Name _____ Account Number _____

Address _____

_____ Postcode _____

Telephone Number_____

Email _____

Payment by: ❏ Cheque ❏ Mastercard ❏ Visa ❏ Postal Order ❏ Maestro

Card no ▢▢▢▢ ▢▢▢▢ ▢▢▢▢ ▢▢▢▢ ▢▢▢

Valid from ▢▢▢▢ Expires ▢▢▢▢ Issue no. ▢▢▢

Security code* ▢▢▢ *Last 3 digits on the reverse of the card. ESSENTIAL IN ORDER TO PROCESS YOUR ORDER — Shaded boxes for Maestro use only

Signature _____ Date _____

All orders must be accompanied by the appropriate payment.

Please send your completed order form to:
BRF, 15 The Chambers, Vineyard, Abingdon OX14 3FE
Tel. 01865 319700 / Fax. 01865 319701 Email: enquiries@brf.org.uk

❏ Please send me further information about BRF publications.

Available from your local Christian bookshop.   BRF is a Registered Charity

About
brf:

BRF is a registered charity and also a limited company, and has been in existence since 1922. Through all that we do—producing resources, providing training, working face-to-face with adults and children, and via the web—we work to resource individuals and church communities in their Christian discipleship through the Bible, prayer and worship.

Our Barnabas children's team works with primary schools and churches to help children under 11, and the adults who work with them, to explore Christianity creatively and to bring the Bible alive.

To find out more about BRF and its core activities and ministries, visit:

www.brf.org.uk
www.barnabasinschools.org.uk
www.barnabasinchurches.org.uk
www.messychurch.org.uk
www.foundations21.org.uk

If you have any questions about BRF and our work, please email us at

enquiries@brf.org.uk

enter